# MONEY MATTE₹S

## A JOURNEY FROM CENTRALIZED CURRENCY TO A DECENTRALIZED ONE



SUBHRADEEP SARKAR

notionpress.com

INDIA • SINGAPORE • MALAYSIA

ISBN
Hardcase 979-8-90451-284-2
Paperback 979-8-90342-943-1

This book is dedicated to my Baba and Maa and to my father-in-law and mother-in-law, sister-in-law and to my entire family and of course to my dear Boni, without her immense support it wouldn't be a reality. Thank you.

# Contents


*Preface* 7

01. What is Money and Why is it Used as Legal Tender 9

02. History and Evolution of Money as a Legal Tender 17

03. Is Money as a Centralised Regulated Currency Worth its Value 25

04. How Money Help You Out From Poverty to a Socio-Economic Status 33

05. Types of Money and Their Usage 45

06. How Different Currencies Gain its Value 53

07. Effect of Money Over Economy 61

08. Money Versus Asset, Which is Better 69

09. Does Money Create Social Gap or Upliftment 73

10. Principals of Money in Globalization and Global Climate Action 81

11. What is Decentralize Financing 91

12. Is Cryptocurrency is the Future 101

13. Concept of Money With Respect to Artificial Intelligence in Labour Market 111

14. Concept of Money With Respect to Research in Space and Medical Technology 121

15. Money, Finance and Blockchain Technology 131

16. Monetary Policy and International Financing Through Organizations 141

17. Block Chian Economy 151

18. How Quantum Cryptography Could Be a Game Changer for Decentralised Financing 163

*Conclusion* *171*

*About the Author* *173*

# Preface

The history of civilization is, in many respects, a history of trust. At the heart of this trust lies money—a concept that has migrated from the tangible weight of gold and salt to the ethereal flicker of digital ledgers. This work examines the profound transformation of money from a mere utility of trade into a definitive instrument of statecraft and social engineering.

In the modern era, the value of a currency is no longer anchored to the scarcity of a metal, but to the stability of the institutions that issue it. This shift toward **fiat currency** represents a pivotal moment in human history; it decoupled economic growth from physical limitations, allowing states to manage economies with unprecedented precision. However, as this text explores, such power is a double-edged sword. While centralized control provides the "standardized framework" necessary for global commerce, it also introduces the complexities of inflation and the heavy hand of monetary policy.

Beyond its role in macroeconomics, this study highlights money as a catalyst for individual liberation. By serving as a store of value that can be directed toward **human capital**, money acts as a bridge across the chasm of generational poverty. It is the fuel for social mobility, transforming labour into opportunity and stability.

As we stand on the precipice of a digital revolution—defined by cryptocurrencies and sovereign digital assets—the definitions of "legal tender" and "state power" are once again being challenged. This work seeks to provide the historical and theoretical context necessary to navigate this evolution, reminding us that while the form of money may change, its fundamental purpose remains the same: a mirror of our collective trust and a tool for our shared future.

# 01

# What is Money and Why is it Used as Legal Tender

Money is any object or record generally accepted as payment for goods and services and the repayment of debts. It functions as a **medium of exchange**, a **unit of account**, and a **store of value**.

## Analysis of Money

To function effectively, money must possess several core characteristics:

- **Fungibility**: Individual units must be interchangeable (e.g., one ₹100 note is worth the same as any other).
- **Durability**: It must withstand repeated use over time without deteriorating.
- **Portability**: It must be easy to carry and transport for transactions.
- **Divisibility**: It must be breakable into smaller units to allow for precise pricing.
- **Scarcity**: Its supply must be limited to maintain value and prevent high inflation.

## Why Money is Used as Legal Tender

**Legal tender** is a specific status assigned to a currency by a government, mandating its acceptance for the settlement of debts.

- **Mandatory Debt Settlement**: By law, a creditor cannot refuse legal tender when offered by a debtor to extinguish a monetary obligation.
- **Economic Stability**: It ensures a uniform, standardized currency across the nation, reducing the confusion and transaction costs associated with multiple competing currencies.
- **Government Authority**: It allows the state to maintain control over the money supply and effectively implement **monetary policy**.
- **Fiat Value**: Most modern money (fiat money) has no intrinsic value; it derives its worth solely because the government declares it legal tender and people have faith in that authority.

## Types of Legal Tender in India

In India, legal tender is governed by the Reserve Bank of India Act, 1934 and the Coinage Act, 2011:

- **Unlimited Legal Tender**: Currency notes (issued by the Reserve Bank of India) can be used to settle debts of any amount.
- **Limited Legal Tender**: Coins (issued by the Government of India) are legal tender only up to specific limits—for example, ₹1 coins and above are legal tender for sums up to ₹1,000.

# Money & Legal Tender

Understanding what money is, why it matters, and how legal tender shapes the Indian economy.

CHAPTER 1 FOUNDATIONS

## What Is Money?

Money is any object or verifiable record that is generally accepted as payment for goods and services, and for the repayment of debts within an economy. While its forms have evolved—from cowrie shells and gold coins to digital wallets—the core purpose of money has remained unchanged for millennia.

To qualify as "money," an instrument must reliably perform **three essential functions** that underpin every modern economy:

### Medium of Exchange

Money eliminates the inefficiency of barter by providing a universally accepted intermediary for buying and selling goods and services.

### Unit of Account

Money provides a common standard for measuring and comparing the value of different goods, services, and assets in the marketplace.

### Store of Value

Money allows individuals to save purchasing power over time, enabling them to defer consumption and plan for future needs.

CHAPTER 2 ANALYSIS OF MONEY

# Core Characteristics of Effective Money

For money to function reliably in any economy, it must possess a set of essential properties. Without these characteristics, trust erodes and the monetary system becomes unstable. Each property plays a critical role in ensuring that money serves its intended purpose across millions of daily transactions.

### Fungibility

Every individual unit of money must be perfectly interchangeable with another of the same denomination. For example, one ₹100 note holds exactly the same value as any other ₹100 note, regardless of its age or condition.

### Durability

Money must be able to withstand repeated physical use over extended periods without significant deterioration. This is why modern currencies use polymer notes and alloyed metals for coins.

### Portability

Money must be convenient to carry and transport. A good currency packs significant value into a small, lightweight form—enabling seamless transactions anywhere.

### Divisibility

It must be possible to break money into smaller units to facilitate precise pricing and change-making. The Indian rupee, for instance, divides into 100 paise.

### Scarcity

The supply of money must be carefully controlled and limited. Without scarcity, money loses its purchasing power, leading to inflation and economic instability.

CHAPTER 3 LEGAL TENDER

# What Is Legal Tender?

**Legal tender** is a special status assigned to a form of currency by the government of a country. When a currency is designated as legal tender, it means that it **must** be accepted for the settlement of monetary debts. A creditor cannot legally refuse legal tender when it is offered by a debtor to discharge an obligation. This designation forms the bedrock of trust in a nation's monetary system.

# Why Money Is Used as Legal Tender

Governments around the world designate specific currencies as legal tender for several compelling reasons. This framework ensures economic order, public confidence, and policy effectiveness.

1

### Mandatory Debt Settlement

By law, a creditor cannot refuse legal tender when it is offered by a debtor to extinguish a monetary obligation. This legal guarantee ensures that all parties in a transaction have a reliable, enforceable means of payment.

2

### Economic Stability

Legal tender ensures a uniform, standardised currency circulates across the entire nation. This eliminates the confusion and high transaction costs that would arise from multiple competing currencies operating simultaneously.

3

### Government Authority

The legal tender framework allows the state to maintain decisive control over the money supply and effectively implement **monetary policy**—managing interest rates, inflation, and overall economic growth.

4

### Fiat Value

Most modern money is **fiat money**—it has no intrinsic value like gold or silver. It derives its worth solely because the government declares it legal tender and citizens place their trust in that authority.

# The Concept of Fiat Money

Unlike commodity money (such as gold coins), **fiat money** possesses no intrinsic material value. A ₹500 note, for instance, is merely a piece of printed paper—its real value stems entirely from the government's declaration and public trust.

This system works because of a powerful social contract: citizens believe the currency will be accepted by others in exchange for goods and services. The moment that collective faith weakens, the currency's value can collapse —as seen in cases of hyperinflation across history.

**Key Insight:** The word "fiat" comes from Latin, meaning "let it be done." Fiat money exists by government decree—not by the value of the material it is made from.

CHAPTER 4 LEGAL TENDER IN INDIA

# Types of Legal Tender in India

In India, the legal tender framework is governed by two key pieces of legislation: the **Reserve Bank of India Act, 1934** and the **Coinage Act, 2011**. Together, they define which instruments must be accepted for transactions and the limits that apply.

## Unlimited vs Limited Legal Tender

Indian law distinguishes between two categories of legal tender, each with different rules regarding the amounts for which they can be used to settle debts.

### Unlimited Legal Tender

**Currency notes** issued by the Reserve Bank of India (RBI) are classified as unlimited legal tender. This means they can be used to settle debts of **any amount**, no matter how large. A payment made entirely in ₹10 notes for a debt of ₹10,00,000 must legally be accepted.

### Limited Legal Tender

**Coins** issued by the Government of India are legal tender only up to specific limits. For instance, coins of ₹1 denomination and above are legal tender for sums up to **₹1,000** only. Beyond that limit, a creditor may lawfully refuse coin-based payments.

These distinctions exist to prevent impractical situations—such as settling a large commercial debt with bags of small-denomination coins—while still ensuring coins remain usable for everyday transactions.

## Who Issues What?

India's monetary instruments are issued by two separate authorities, each governed by distinct legislation. Understanding this distinction is essential to grasping how the Indian monetary system operates.

| 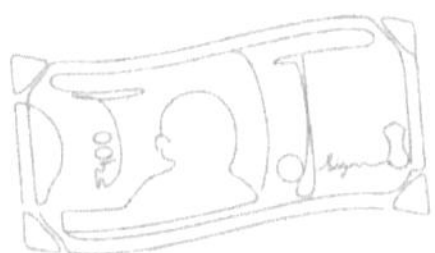 |  |
|---|---|
| **RESERVE BANK OF INDIA** | **GOVERNMENT OF INDIA** |
| ISSUES CURRENCY NOTES | ISSUES COINS |
| UNDER RBI ACT 1934 | UNDER COINAGE ACT 2011 |
| UNLIMITED LEGAL TENDER | LIMITED LEGAL TENDER (UP TO ₹1000) |
| DENOMINATIONS ₹2 TO ₹2000 | DENOMINATIONS 50 PAISE TO ₹20 |
| CONTAINS GOVERNOR'S SIGNATURE | MINTED AT GOVT MINTS |

## Key Takeaways

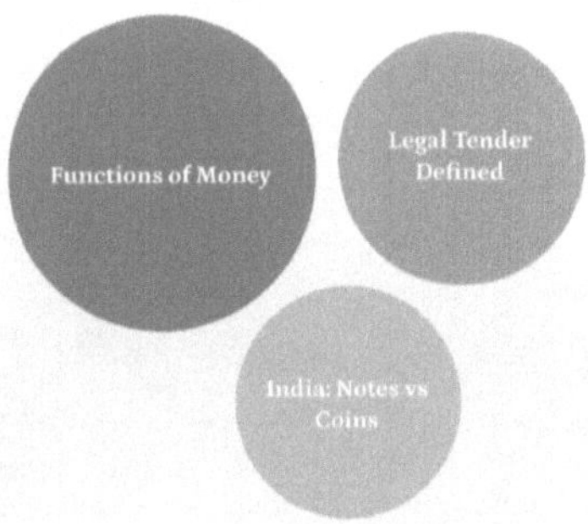


Money is far more than coins and paper—it is the foundation of economic trust. Legal tender laws ensure that every citizen has a reliable, government-backed means of settling obligations, maintaining stability and confidence across the entire economy.

# 02

# History and Evolution of Money as a Legal Tender

The history and evolution of money as legal tender is the transition from objects with intrinsic value to government-mandated tokens of trust. While money has existed for over 5,000 years, its status as "legal tender"—meaning it **must** be accepted by law to settle debts—solidified as central authorities took control of currency issuance.

## Evolutionary Stages of Money

- **Barter System (Pre-6000 BCE)**: Direct exchange of goods (e.g., wheat for shoes) without a standardized medium.
    - Limited by the "double coincidence of wants".
- **Commodity Money (c. 3000 BCE)**: Items with intrinsic value, such as salt, cowrie shells, and livestock, served as early money.
    - Accepted based on perceived utility and common consent.
- **Metallic Money & Coinage (c. $7^{th}$ Century BCE)**: Standardized metal coins (gold, silver, electrum) were first minted in **Lydia** (modern Turkey).
    - Introduction of official seals guaranteed weight and value, marking the birth of "official" currency.

- **Representative Paper Money (7$^{th}$–11$^{th}$ Century CE)**: China's **Tang and Song Dynasties** introduced paper receipts backed by precious metals.
    - In Europe, 17$^{th}$-century goldsmiths issued receipts that evolved into modern banknotes.
- **Fiat Money (1971–Present)**: Money not backed by physical commodities but by government decree (fiat).
    - The "Nixon Shock" in 1971 ended the gold standard, making the U.S. dollar and other national currencies free-floating fiat money.
- **Digital & Crypto Era (Late 20$^{th}$ Century–Present)**: Transition to electronic records, plastic cards (debit/credit), and decentralized cryptocurrencies like **Bitcoin** (2009).

## Timeline of Legal Tender Development

| Era | Milestone | Significance |
|---|---|---|
| **c. 600 BCE** | First Minted Coins (Lydia) | Standardized value established by a central authority. |
| **1694** | Bank of England Established | First central bank to issue widely accepted banknotes. |
| **1861/1862** | Legal Tender Acts (US & India) | Mandated paper currency as "legal tender" to settle all public and private debts. |

| Era | Milestone | Significance |
|---|---|---|
| **1934** | RBI Act (India) | Granted the **Reserve Bank of India** sole authority to issue banknotes as legal tender. |
| **1971** | End of Gold Standard | Shift to pure fiat systems where money derives value from legal mandate and trust. |
| **2020s** | CBDC Implementation | Central banks (e.g., India's **e-Rupee**) explore digital legal tender to modernize fiat money. |

## Key Legislative Milestones in India

- **Paper Currency Act (1861)**: Abolished private bank notes, giving the government exclusive rights to issue currency.
- **Coinage Act (1906/2011)**: Established coins as **limited legal tender** (accepted only up to specified amounts).
- **RBI Act (1934)**: Formally declared RBI-issued notes as **unlimited legal tender** anywhere in India.

## Key Takeaways

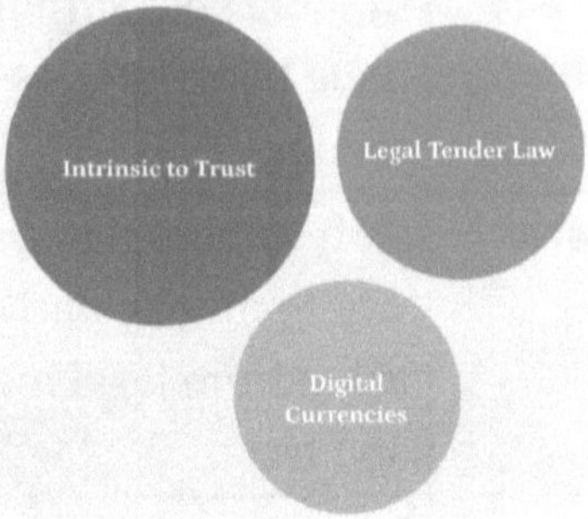


The story of money is ultimately a story of **trust** — from trusting the weight of gold to trusting the decree of governments, and now, trusting the code behind digital currencies. Each evolution reflects society's growing sophistication in organising economic life.

CHAPTER 3 INDIA FOCUS

## Key Legislative Milestones in India

### Paper Currency Act (1861)

Abolished private bank notes, giving the **government exclusive rights** to issue currency across India.

### Coinage Act (1906/2011)

Established coins as **limited legal tender** — accepted only up to specified amounts for transactions.

### RBI Act (1934)

Formally declared RBI-issued notes as **unlimited legal tender** anywhere in India, granting the Reserve Bank sole authority over banknote issuance.

CHAPTER 2 KEY MILESTONES

# Timeline of Legal Tender Development

From the first minted coins to digital currencies — the critical milestones that shaped money as we know it.

| Era | Milestone | Significance |
|---|---|---|
| c. 600 BCE | First Minted Coins (Lydia) | Standardised value established by a central authority |
| 1694 | Bank of England Established | First central bank to issue widely accepted banknotes |
| 1861/1862 | Legal Tender Acts (US & India) | Mandated paper currency as "legal tender" for all public and private debts |
| 1934 | RBI Act (India) | Granted the Reserve Bank of India sole authority to issue banknotes as legal tender |
| 1971 | End of Gold Standard | Shift to pure fiat systems — money derives value from legal mandate and trust |
| 2020s | CBDC Implementation | Central banks (e.g., India's e-Rupee) explore digital legal tender |

# The Digital & Crypto Era

The late 20th century ushered in a new paradigm — money as pure digital information.

### Electronic Records

Debit and credit cards transformed transactions into electronic records

### Cryptocurrencies

Decentralised currencies like **Bitcoin (2009)** challenged traditional money

### CBDCs

Central banks now explore digital legal tender like India's **e-Rupee**

TURNING POINT

# The Fiat Money Revolution

### 1971 – The Nixon Shock

Fiat money is currency **not backed by physical commodities** but by government decree (*fiat*). The pivotal moment came in **1971** when President Nixon ended the gold standard, making the U.S. dollar and other national currencies free-floating fiat money.

From this point, money derived its value purely from **legal mandate and public trust** — not from gold reserves or any tangible asset. This shift fundamentally redefined what "legal tender" means in the modern world.

# The Rise of Paper Money

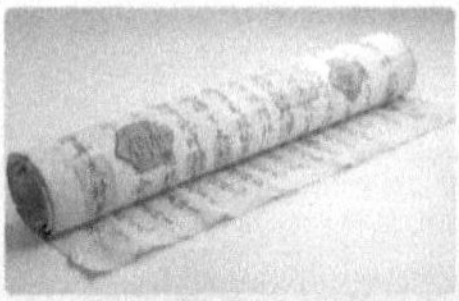

### China's Innovation (7th–11th Century CE)

China's **Tang and Song Dynasties** introduced paper receipts backed by precious metals — the world's first paper money. These notes were lighter, easier to transport, and revolutionised commerce across Asia.

### Europe's Banknotes (17th Century)

In Europe, 17th-century **goldsmiths** issued receipts for deposited gold that evolved into modern banknotes. These receipts circulated as money, forming the foundation of the modern banking system.

## The Birth of Coinage

C. 7TH CENTURY BCE

### Metallic Money & Standardised Coins

Standardised metal coins made of **gold, silver, and electrum** were first minted in **Lydia** (modern-day Turkey). The introduction of official seals guaranteed weight and value, marking the birth of "official" currency.

This was a revolutionary moment — for the first time, a **central authority** vouched for the value of money, laying the groundwork for the concept of legal tender.

**Why It Mattered**

- Standardised weight and purity
- Official seals built public trust
- Enabled long-distance trade
- Central authority guaranteed value

## Barter & Commodity Money

### Barter System (Pre-6000 BCE)

Direct exchange of goods — wheat for shoes, livestock for tools. This system was severely limited by the **"double coincidence of wants"**: both parties had to desire what the other offered at the same time.

### Commodity Money (c. 3000 BCE)

Items with intrinsic value — **salt, cowrie shells, and livestock** — served as early money. These were accepted based on perceived utility and common consent, solving many limitations of barter.

# The Journey of Money Through the Ages

Money has undergone a remarkable transformation — from simple barter to digital currencies. Each stage reflects humanity's growing need for standardised, trustworthy mediums of exchange. While money has existed for millennia, its status as **"legal tender"** — meaning it **must** be accepted by law to settle debts — solidified as central authorities took control of currency issuance.

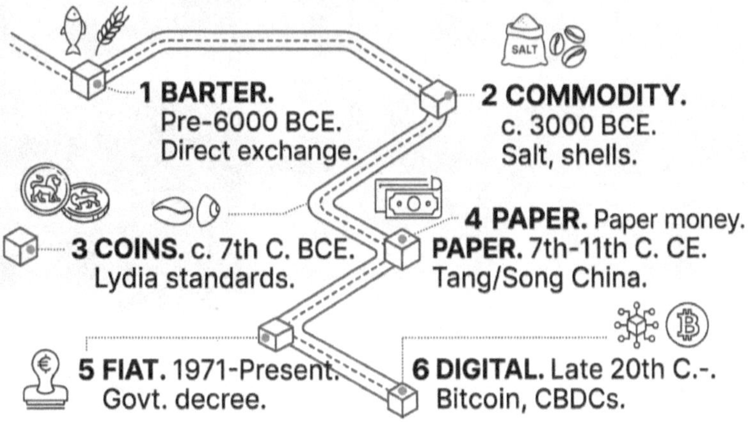

## The History & Evolution of Money as Legal Tender

From objects with intrinsic value to government-mandated tokens of trust — tracing over 5,000 years of monetary evolution and the rise of "legal tender" as central authorities took control of currency issuance.

# 03

# Is Money as a Centralised Regulated Currency Worth its Value

Whether money as a centralized regulated currency is "worth its value" depends on your priority: **stability and wide acceptance** versus **scarcity and privacy**. Modern fiat currency has no intrinsic value; its worth is derived entirely from **public trust** in the issuing government and its legal status as tender.

## The Case for Centralized Currency (Pros)

- **Stability & Management**: Central banks use monetary policy (adjusting interest rates and money supply) to manage inflation and stabilize the economy during crises.
- **Universal Acceptance**: It is mandated by law (legal tender) for all debts, public and private, and must be accepted for tax payments, ensuring constant demand.
- **Transaction Efficiency**: Modern fiat systems are cost-effective to produce and facilitate complex global trade more efficiently than commodity-based systems like the gold standard.
- **Consumer Protection**: Regulated currencies are backed by the "full faith and credit" of the state, providing a safety net that decentralized assets lack.

## The Case Against Centralized Currency (Cons)

- **Inflation Risk**: Because the supply is not fixed, governments may print excessive money to cover deficits, which can lead to a rapid loss of purchasing power or even hyperinflation (e.g., Zimbabwe or Venezuela).
- **Susceptibility to Manipulation**: Centralized control allows for political or economic manipulation of interest rates and money supply, which may not always align with the long-term interests of savers.
- **Lack of Privacy**: Digital centralized currencies (like the Digital Rupee) allow for total government oversight of transactions, reducing the anonymity found in cash or decentralized crypto.
- **Single Point of Failure**: A collapse in government stability or a major cybersecurity breach in centralized ledgers can jeopardize the entire financial system.

## Comparison: Centralized vs. Decentralized

| Feature | Centralized (Fiat/CBDC) | Decentralized (Crypto) |
|---|---|---|
| **Backing** | Government Authority/ Economy | Mathematical Consensus/ Market Demand |
| **Supply** | Flexible (Managed by Central Bank) | Often Fixed (e.g., Bitcoin) |
| **Trust** | Institutional Trust | Algorithmic/Trustless |
| **Volatility** | Generally Low (Controlled) | Often High (Market-driven) |

Centralized currency remains "worth its value" primarily because of its **utility as a medium of exchange** and the legal framework that forces its adoption. However, its "store of value" function is continuously challenged by inflation, leading some to seek decentralized alternatives for long-term wealth preservation.

## The Verdict

Centralized currency remains "worth its value" primarily because of its **utility as a medium of exchange** and the legal framework that forces its adoption.

However, its **"store of value" function** is continuously challenged by inflation, leading some to seek decentralised alternatives for long-term wealth preservation.

### Medium of Exchange

Fiat excels here — universal, efficient, legally mandated

### Store of Value

Increasingly contested — inflation erodes purchasing power over time

CHAPTER 4 COMPARISON

## Centralized vs. Decentralized

How do traditional fiat currencies and CBDCs stack up against decentralised cryptocurrencies across key dimensions?

| Feature | Centralized (Fiat/CBDC) | Decentralized (Crypto) |
|---|---|---|
| **Backing** | Government Authority / Economy | Mathematical Consensus / Market Demand |
| **Supply** | Flexible (Managed by Central Bank) | Often Fixed (e.g., Bitcoin) |
| **Trust** | Institutional Trust | Algorithmic / Trustless |
| **Volatility** | Generally Low (Controlled) | Often High (Market-driven) |

## Privacy & Systemic Vulnerabilities

### Lack of Privacy

Digital centralised currencies (like the Digital Rupee) allow for **total government oversight** of transactions, reducing the anonymity found in cash or decentralised crypto.

### Single Point of Failure

A collapse in government stability or a major **cybersecurity breach** in centralised ledgers can jeopardise the entire financial system.

## Inflation & Manipulation Risks

### Inflation Risk

Because the supply is not fixed, governments may print excessive money to cover deficits, leading to rapid loss of purchasing power or even **hyperinflation** — as seen in Zimbabwe and Venezuela.

### Susceptibility to Manipulation

Centralised control allows for political or economic manipulation of interest rates and money supply, which may not always align with the **long-term interests of savers**.

CHAPTER 3 THE CASE AGAINST

# The Case Against Centralized Currency

Despite its advantages, centralized currency carries significant risks that critics argue undermine its long-term reliability.

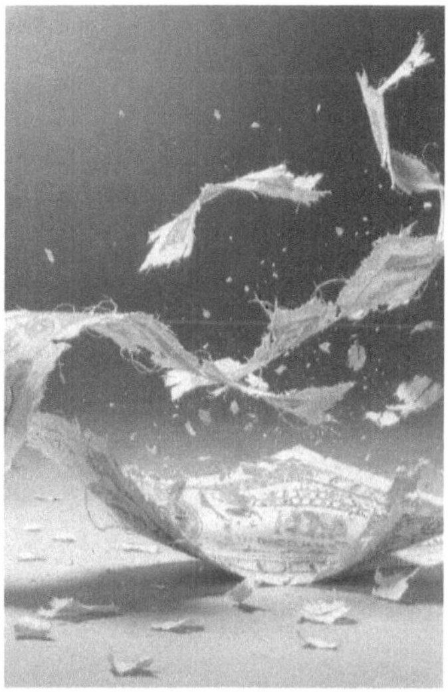

## Consumer Protection

### Backed by the State

Regulated currencies are backed by the **"full faith and credit"** of the state, providing a safety net that decentralised assets lack.

- This institutional backing means depositors are protected through schemes like deposit insurance — a layer of security absent in most decentralised systems.

## Stability, Acceptance & Efficiency

### Stability & Management

Central banks use monetary policy — adjusting interest rates and money supply — to manage inflation and stabilise the economy during crises.

### Universal Acceptance

Mandated by law as legal tender for all debts, public and private, and required for tax payments — ensuring constant demand.

### Transaction Efficiency

Modern fiat systems are cost-effective to produce and facilitate complex global trade more efficiently than commodity-based systems like the gold standard.

CHAPTER 2 THE CASE FOR

# The Case for Centralized Currency

Centralized currencies offer powerful advantages that have made them the backbone of global economies for decades.

CHAPTER 1 FOUNDATION

# The Nature of Modern Money

Modern fiat currency has **no intrinsic value**. Its worth is derived entirely from **public trust** in the issuing government and its legal status as tender.

Whether money as a centralized regulated currency is "worth its value" depends on your priority: **stability and wide acceptance** versus **scarcity and privacy**.

This fundamental question shapes how nations, institutions, and individuals think about wealth, savings, and the future of finance.

**Key Insight**

Fiat currency's value is a social contract — it works because we collectively agree it does.

## Is Centralized Currency Worth Its Value?

Exploring the tension between **stability and wide acceptance** versus **scarcity and privacy** in the modern monetary system.

# 04

# How Money Help You Out From Poverty to a Socio-Economic Status

Money serves as the primary engine for transitioning from poverty to a higher socio-economic status by providing the means to invest in **human capital**, **productive assets**, and **financial safety nets**. While poverty is often a "trap" where daily survival consumes all resources, the injection of capital—whether through increased income, credit, or cash transfers—enables individuals to shift from labour-intensive survival to business and service-oriented roles.

## 1. Breaking the Poverty Trap through Investment

Financial resources allow individuals to move beyond hand-to-mouth existence by funding growth-oriented activities:

- **Human Capital**: Money pays for education and vocational training, which are the most consistent predictors of upward mobility. Higher education levels lead to better-paying occupations and improved decision-making skills.
- **Productive Assets**: Access to capital enables the poor to start or expand small businesses (e.g., tailoring, livestock, or agricultural production), which generates sustainable, long-term income rather than daily wages.

- **Preventative Maintenance**: Wealth allows for upfront spending on healthcare and home repairs, preventing minor issues from becoming catastrophic expenses that would otherwise trigger a return to poverty.

## 2. The Role of Financial Inclusion

Transitioning status requires moving from informal to formal financial systems:

- **Safe Savings**: Formal accounts provide a secure way to accumulate resources for large future investments like housing or education.
- **Access to Credit**: Affordable credit—as opposed to predatory high-interest informal loans—allows for risk-taking and business scaling.
- **Insurance**: Financial products like inclusive insurance shield vulnerable households from "shocks" (illness, natural disasters) that could wipe out accumulated wealth.

## 3. Socio-Economic Status (SES) and Quality of Life

As income and wealth increase, they fundamentally alter an individual's social position and well-being:

- **Living Standards**: Higher income is directly correlated with better housing (moving from "kutcha" or temporary houses to "pucca" or permanent structures) and improved nutrition.
- **Psychological Agency**: Moving out of poverty reduces chronic stress and increases a sense of "subjective SES"—the feeling of having choices and agency, which is a strong predictor of overall life satisfaction.
- **Social Capital**: Increased wealth often helps build stronger social networks and community connections, which further facilitate access to better jobs and opportunities.

## 4. Barriers and Multipliers

- **Gender and Equality**: Money has a greater impact on poverty reduction when it is directed toward women, as they are often more likely to invest in family health and education.
- **Complementary Services**: Financial assistance is most effective when paired with "social services," such as healthcare access and financial literacy training, to ensure wealth is managed sustainably.

# Key Takeaways

1 **Money breaks the poverty trap**

Investment in education, productive assets, and preventative health shifts individuals from survival to sustainable growth.

2 **Financial inclusion is essential**

Safe savings, affordable credit, and insurance protect and grow accumulated wealth.

3 **Rising income transforms lives**

Better housing, reduced stress, greater agency, and stronger social networks follow increased wealth.

4 **Equity and services multiply impact**

Directing resources to women and pairing finance with healthcare and literacy training maximises outcomes.

## The Complete Framework

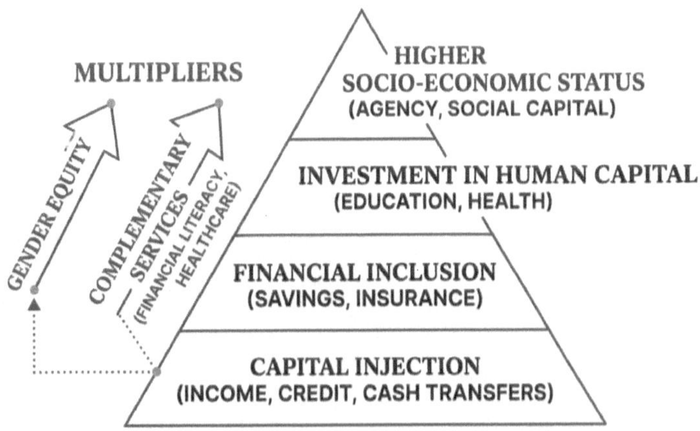


Each layer builds upon the one below. Capital injection forms the foundation, financial inclusion provides the tools, investment creates growth, and the result is a fundamentally transformed socio-economic position—amplified by gender equity and complementary services.

## Complementary Services Maximise Impact

Financial assistance is most effective when paired with **social services** to ensure wealth is managed sustainably. Money alone is necessary but not sufficient—it must be accompanied by the knowledge and infrastructure to use it wisely.

### Healthcare Access

Ensuring families can maintain health to remain productive and avoid catastrophic medical expenses.

### Financial Literacy

Training in budgeting, saving, and investment ensures that new wealth is managed sustainably over time.

### Social Safety Nets

Insurance and support programmes protect against shocks that could reverse hard-won economic gains.

## Gender Equity as a Poverty Multiplier

Money has a **greater impact on poverty reduction** when directed toward women, as they are often more likely to invest in family health and education. Gender-focused financial empowerment creates ripple effects across entire communities.

### Women Receive Capital

Targeted financial assistance and microloans directed to women

### Family Investment

Women invest disproportionately in children's health and education

### Community Uplift

Healthier, better-educated families strengthen the entire community

CHAPTER 4

# Barriers & Multipliers

## The Wellbeing Multiplier Effect

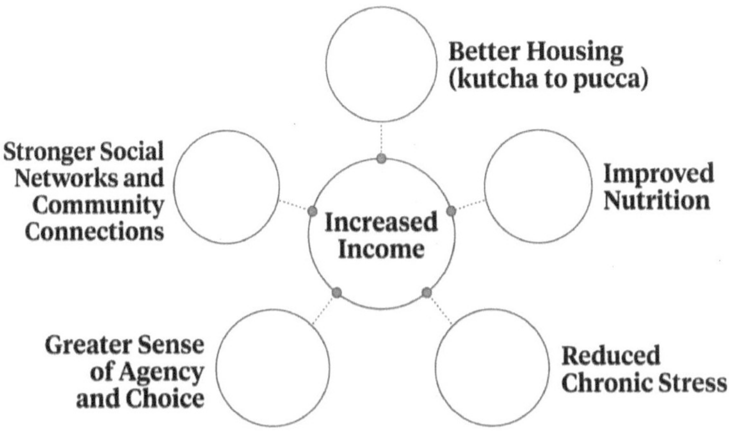


Each improvement reinforces the others—better nutrition supports health, reduced stress improves decision-making, and stronger networks open doors to new opportunities, creating a self-reinforcing cycle of upward mobility.

## How Income Transforms Quality of Life

As income and wealth increase, they fundamentally alter an individual's social position and well-being across multiple dimensions.

### Living Standards

Higher income correlates directly with better housing—moving from "kutcha" (temporary) to "pucca" (permanent) structures—and improved nutrition.

### Psychological Agency

Moving out of poverty reduces chronic stress and increases "subjective SES"—the feeling of having choices, a strong predictor of life satisfaction.

### Social Capital

Increased wealth builds stronger social networks and community connections, facilitating access to better jobs and opportunities.

CHAPTER 3

# Rising Socio-Economic Status

## Moving from Informal to Formal Finance

Transitioning socio-economic status requires access to formal financial systems. Without safe savings, affordable credit, and insurance, accumulated wealth remains fragile and vulnerable to shocks.

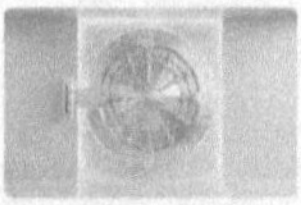

### Safe Savings

Formal accounts provide a secure way to accumulate resources for large future investments like housing or education.

### Access to Credit

Affordable credit—as opposed to predatory high-interest informal loans—allows for risk-taking and business scaling.

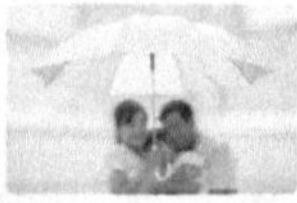

### Insurance

Inclusive insurance shields vulnerable households from shocks—illness, natural disasters—that could wipe out accumulated wealth.

CHAPTER 2

# Financial Inclusion

# From Survival to Sustainability

The shift from daily-wage labour to business ownership represents a fundamental change in economic trajectory. Capital investment creates a virtuous cycle of growth.

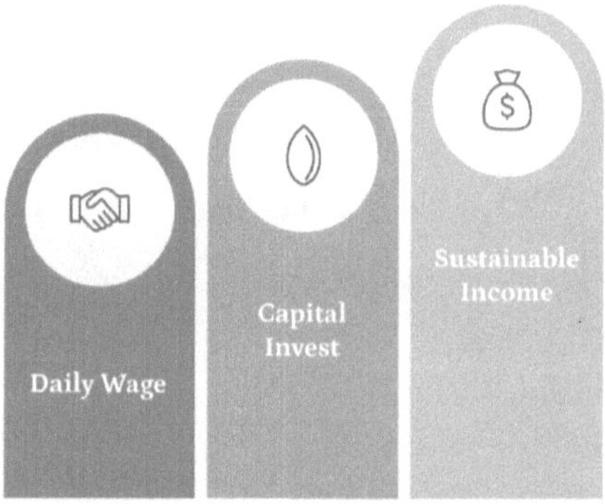


Each stage builds upon the previous one—once basic survival is secured, resources can be redirected toward growth-oriented activities that compound over time.

# Investing in Human Capital

Financial resources allow individuals to move beyond hand-to-mouth existence by funding growth-oriented activities. **Education and vocational training** are the most consistent predictors of upward mobility.

### Education

Money pays for schooling and vocational training, leading to better-paying occupations and improved decision-making skills.

### Productive Assets

Access to capital enables the poor to start or expand small businesses—tailoring, livestock, agriculture—generating sustainable, long-term income rather than daily wages.

### Preventative Maintenance

Wealth allows upfront spending on healthcare and home repairs, preventing minor issues from becoming catastrophic expenses that trigger a return to poverty.

CHAPTER 1

# Breaking the Poverty Trap

OVERVIEW

## The Journey from Poverty to Prosperity

Poverty is often a "trap" where daily survival consumes all resources. The injection of capital—whether through increased income, credit, or cash transfers—enables individuals to shift from labour-intensive survival to business and service-oriented roles.

Money serves as the primary engine for this transition by providing the means to invest in **human capital**, **productive assets**, and **financial safety nets**.

01

### Breaking the Poverty Trap

Investment in education, assets, and health

02

### Financial Inclusion

Moving from informal to formal financial systems

03

### Rising Socio-Economic Status

Improved living standards, agency, and social capital

04

### Barriers & Multipliers

Gender equity and complementary services

# Money as the Engine of Upward Mobility

How financial resources break the poverty trap and unlock a higher socio-economic status through investment, inclusion, and opportunity.

# 05

# Types of Money and Their Usage

In modern economics, money is generally classified into four primary types, each defined by its source of value and specific usage within the financial system.

## 1. Commodity Money

Commodity money is the oldest form of currency, deriving its value from the **intrinsic worth** of the physical material it is made of.

- **Source of Value:** The material itself has utility outside of being used as money (e.g., gold, silver, salt, or copper).
- **Usage:**
- Historically used as a primary medium of exchange to simplify barter systems.
- Serves as a reliable **store of value** because the underlying commodity retains its worth even if a government fails.
- Today, it is largely used for investment (bullion) rather than daily commerce.

## 2. Fiat Money

Fiat money is the dominant form of currency in the modern world, issued by governments and declared as **legal tender**.

- **Source of Value:** It has no intrinsic value; its worth is derived entirely from government decree and the public's trust in the issuing authority.
- **Usage:**
- The primary medium for **daily transactions**, such as buying groceries or paying bills.
- Used by central banks as a tool for **monetary policy**, allowing them to control the money supply to manage inflation and economic growth.
- Examples include the US Dollar and the Indian Rupee.

## 3. Fiduciary Money

Fiduciary money refers to payment instruments that are accepted based on the **trust** between the payer and the payee, rather than a government mandate.

- **Source of Value:** The confidence that the issuer will exchange the instrument for fiat or commodity money upon request.
- **Usage:**
- Facilitates transactions without the immediate transfer of physical cash.
- Used extensively in business for large or remote payments.
- Common examples include **cheques**, drafts, and promissory notes.

## 4. Commercial Bank Money

Also known as "bank money," this type represents claims against financial institutions that can be used to purchase goods and services.

- **Source of Value:** Created through **fractional reserve banking**, where banks issue loans that exceed the physical currency they hold.
- **Usage:**
- Accounts for over 90% of the money supply in developed economies.
- Used for **electronic transfers**, debit card payments, and online banking.
- Functions as the primary mechanism for credit creation in the economy.

## Summary of Money Types and Usage

| Type | Intrinsic Value? | Legal Tender? | Primary Modern Usage |
|---|---|---|---|
| **Commodity** | Yes | Sometimes | Investment, store of value |
| **Fiat** | No | Yes | Daily commerce, govt. policy |
| **Fiduciary** | No | No | Trusted payment (cheques) |
| **Commercial Bank** | No | No | Electronic/digital transactions |

## Key Takeaways

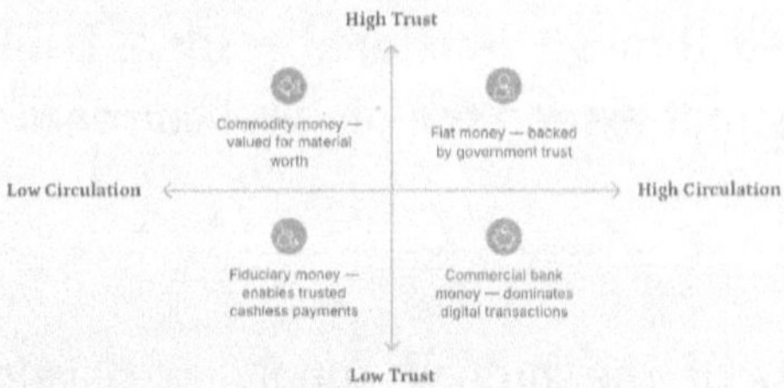


Understanding these four types of money — commodity, fiat, fiduciary, and commercial bank — is essential for grasping how value is created, stored, and exchanged in modern economies.

## Where Value Comes From

The fundamental distinction between money types lies in their **source of value** — from physical material to government authority to interpersonal trust to institutional claims.

### Material Worth

**Commodity money** derives value from the physical substance itself — gold, silver, or copper have utility beyond their role as currency.

### Government Decree

**Fiat money** holds value because a government declares it legal tender and the public trusts the issuing authority.

### Mutual Trust

**Fiduciary money** is accepted based on confidence that the issuer will honour the instrument and exchange it for real value.

### Institutional Claims

**Commercial bank money** is created through fractional reserve banking — claims against banks that power over 90% of the money supply.

## The Evolution of Money

Money has evolved from tangible commodities to increasingly abstract and trust-based forms. This progression reflects growing economic complexity and technological advancement.

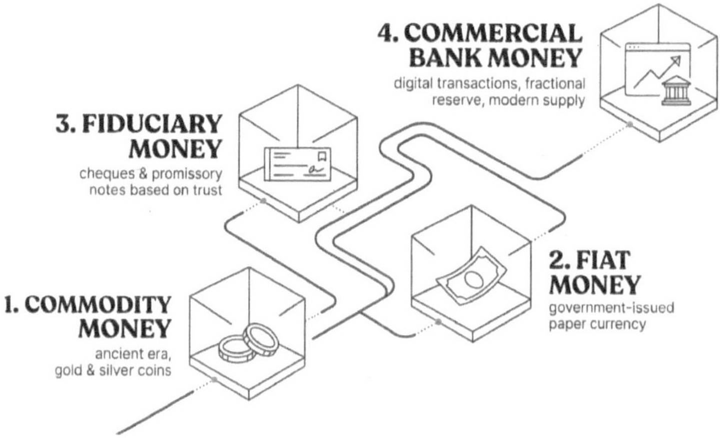


COMPARISON

## How the Four Types Compare

Each type of money differs in intrinsic value, legal tender status, and primary modern usage. The table below summarises these key distinctions.

| Type | Intrinsic Value? | Legal Tender? | Primary Modern Usage |
|---|---|---|---|
| Commodity | Yes | Sometimes | Investment, store of value |
| Fiat | No | Yes | Daily commerce, govt. policy |
| Fiduciary | No | No | Trusted payment (cheques) |
| Commercial Bank | No | No | Electronic/digital transactions |

TYPE 4

## Commercial Bank Money

Also known as **"bank money,"** this type represents claims against financial institutions that can be used to purchase goods and services. It is created through **fractional reserve banking**, where banks issue loans that exceed the physical currency they hold.

**90%+ of Money Supply**

Accounts for over 90% of the money supply in developed economies.

**Electronic Transfers**

Used for debit card payments, online banking, and digital transactions.

**Credit Creation**

Functions as the primary mechanism for credit creation in the economy.

TYPE 3

## Fiduciary Money

Fiduciary money refers to payment instruments accepted based on the **trust between the payer and the payee**, rather than a government mandate. Its value comes from the confidence that the issuer will exchange the instrument for fiat or commodity money upon request.

**Cheques**

Written orders directing a bank to pay a specific amount from the drawer's account.

**Drafts**

Instruments used extensively in business for large or remote payments between parties.

**Promissory Notes**

Written promises to pay a specified sum at a future date, facilitating transactions without immediate cash transfer.

TYPE 2

## Fiat Money

Fiat money is the **dominant form of currency** in the modern world, issued by governments and declared as legal tender. It has **no intrinsic value** — its worth is derived entirely from government decree and the public's trust in the issuing authority.

### Key Uses

- The **primary medium for daily transactions** — buying groceries, paying bills
- Used by central banks as a tool for **monetary policy**, controlling money supply to manage inflation and economic growth
- Examples include the **US Dollar** and the **Indian Rupee**

### Source of Value

Government decree + public trust in the issuing authority. No physical commodity backs it.

TYPE 1

## Commodity Money

Commodity money is the **oldest form of currency**, deriving its value from the intrinsic worth of the physical material it is made of. The material itself has utility outside of being used as money — examples include **gold, silver, salt, and copper**.

### Medium of Exchange

Historically used to simplify barter systems by providing a universally accepted standard of trade.

### Store of Value

The underlying commodity retains its worth even if a government fails, making it a reliable long-term asset.

### Modern Usage

Today, it is largely used for **investment (bullion)** rather than daily commerce.

OVERVIEW

## How Money Is Classified

In modern economics, money is generally classified into **four primary types**, each defined by its source of value and specific usage within the financial system. Understanding these distinctions is essential for grasping how economies function, how value is stored, and how transactions are facilitated across the globe.

**Commodity**
Value from material

**Fiat**
Value from decree

**Fiduciary**
Value from trust

**Commercial Bank**
Value from claims

## The Four Types of Money

Understanding how money is classified in modern economics — from ancient commodities to digital bank transactions.

# 06

# How Different Currencies Gain its Value

Currencies gain value primarily through the economic principle of **supply and demand**. In a floating exchange rate system, when demand for a currency exceeds its supply, its value appreciates relative to other currencies.

## 1. Interest Rate Differentials

- **Higher interest rates** typically attract foreign capital as investors seek better returns on assets like government bonds.
- To invest, these foreign entities must sell their own currency and buy the local one, driving up **demand** and valuation.
- Conversely, lower rates often lead to capital flight and currency depreciation.

## 2. Inflation Rates

- Countries with consistently **lower inflation** rates tend to have stronger currencies.
- Low inflation preserves a currency's **purchasing power**, making its goods and services cheaper and more attractive to foreign buyers compared to high-inflation nations.
- High inflation erodes value, making exports less competitive and reducing global demand for that currency.

## 3. Trade Balance (Current Account)

- A **trade surplus** (exporting more than importing) creates a net inflow of foreign currency.
- Foreign buyers must purchase the exporting nation's currency to pay for goods, which increases demand.
- A persistent **trade deficit** requires a country to sell more of its own currency to buy foreign goods, leading to depreciation.

## 4. Economic Performance and Stability

- **GDP Growth**: Robust economic growth signals a healthy economy, encouraging foreign direct investment (FDI) and increasing currency demand.
- **Political Stability**: Investors seek "safe havens" with stable governments; political unrest or uncertainty can trigger capital flight and devalue a currency.
- **Public Debt**: High levels of national debt can deter investors due to fears of default or future inflation, weakening the currency.

## 5. Central Bank Intervention

- **Market Operations**: Central banks can artificially increase their currency's value by using foreign reserves to buy back their own currency from the market, reducing supply.
- **Fixed/Pegged Rates**: Some nations tie their currency value to a "peg" (like the US Dollar) and actively trade to maintain that specific exchange rate.

## 6. Market Sentiment and Speculation

- **Trader Sentiment**: If traders believe a currency will rise in the future, they buy it now, which can create a self-fulfilling prophecy of appreciation.

- **Safe-Haven Status**: During global crises, investors flock to perceived stable currencies like the **US Dollar**, **Swiss Franc**, or **Japanese Yen**, causing them to gain value regardless of local economic data.

## Key Takeaways

1 **Supply & Demand Rules**

Currency value is fundamentally driven by how much the world demands it relative to its supply.

2 **Multiple Forces at Play**

Interest rates, inflation, trade balances, economic stability, central bank actions, and market sentiment all interact to shape currency movements.

3 **Perception Matters**

Beyond hard data, trader psychology and safe-haven flows can move currencies — making sentiment as powerful as fundamentals.

## How the Six Drivers Connect

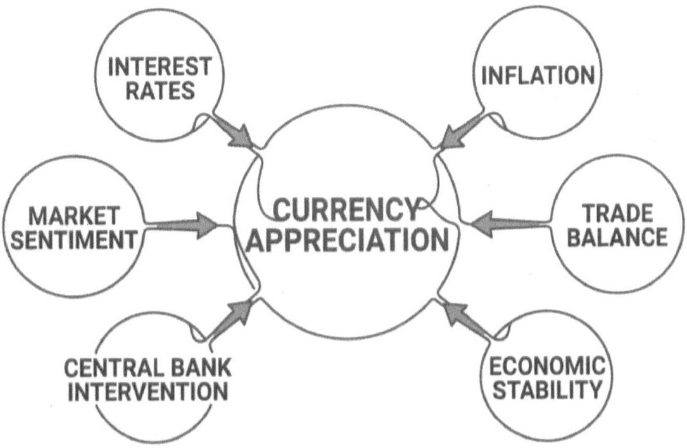


No single factor works in isolation. These six drivers interact continuously, shaping the global supply and demand dynamics that ultimately determine a currency's value on the world stage.

DRIVER 6

## Market Sentiment & Speculation

### Trader Sentiment

If traders believe a currency will rise in the future, they buy it now — creating a **self-fulfilling prophecy** of appreciation that drives real value gains.

### Safe-Haven Status

During global crises, investors flock to perceived stable currencies like the **US Dollar, Swiss Franc, or Japanese Yen**, causing them to gain value regardless of local economic data.

DRIVER 5

## Central Bank Intervention

1

### Market Operations

Central banks can artificially increase their currency's value by using **foreign reserves** to buy back their own currency from the market, reducing supply.

2

### Fixed/Pegged Rates

Some nations tie their currency value to a "peg" (like the US Dollar) and actively trade to maintain that specific exchange rate.

DRIVER 4

## Economic Performance & Stability

### GDP Growth

Robust economic growth signals a healthy economy, encouraging foreign direct investment (FDI) and increasing currency demand.

### Political Stability

Investors seek "safe havens" with stable governments. Political unrest or uncertainty can trigger capital flight and devalue a currency.

### Public Debt

High levels of national debt deter investors due to fears of default or future inflation, weakening the currency.

DRIVER 3

## Trade Balance (Current Account)

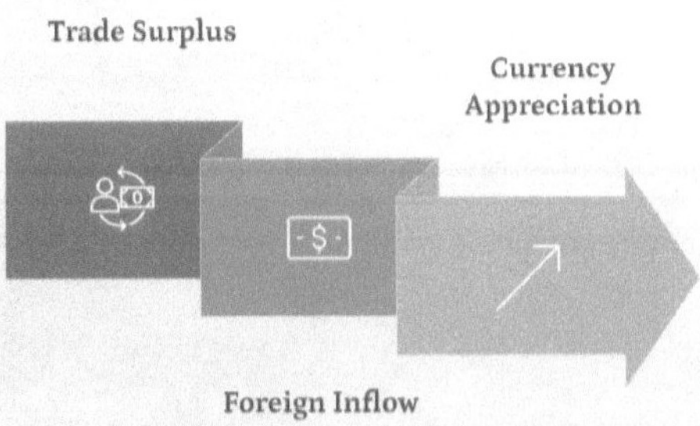


A **trade surplus** creates a net inflow of foreign currency — foreign buyers must purchase the exporting nation's currency to pay for goods. A persistent **trade deficit**, however, requires a country to sell more of its own currency to buy foreign goods, leading to depreciation.

DRIVER 2

## Inflation Rates

### Low Inflation = Stronger Currency

Countries with consistently lower inflation tend to have stronger currencies. Low inflation preserves purchasing power, making goods and services cheaper and more attractive to foreign buyers.

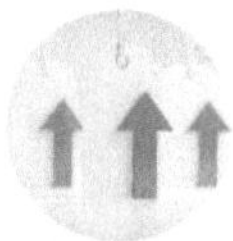

### High Inflation = Erosion

High inflation erodes value, making exports less competitive and reducing global demand for that currency. This creates a downward spiral of depreciation.

DRIVER 1

## Interest Rate Differentials

### Attracting Foreign Capital

Higher interest rates attract foreign investors seeking better returns on assets like government bonds. To invest, they must sell their own currency and buy the local one — driving up demand and valuation.

### The Flip Side

Conversely, lower rates often lead to **capital flight** and currency depreciation, as investors move funds to higher-yielding markets elsewhere.

OVERVIEW

## The Foundation: Supply & Demand

Currencies gain value primarily through the economic principle of **supply and demand**. In a floating exchange rate system, when demand for a currency exceeds its supply, its value appreciates relative to other currencies.

Six key forces drive this dynamic — each influencing how much the world wants (or avoids) a particular currency.

**Six Key Drivers**

01 **Interest Rates**

02 **Inflation**

03 **Trade Balance**

04 **Economic Stability**

05 **Central Banks**

06 **Market Sentiment**

## How Currencies Gain Value

Understanding the economic forces behind currency appreciation — from interest rates and inflation to trade balances and market psychology.

# 07

# Effect of Money Over Economy

The effect of money on the economy is a complex interplay between the total amount of money available (money supply) and macroeconomic variables like inflation, interest rates, and overall growth. Central banks, such as the Reserve Bank of India (RBI), manage this supply to maintain a balance between stimulating development and preventing economic overheating.

## 1. Influence on Key Economic Indicators

- **Interest Rates**: There is an inverse relationship between money supply and interest rates.
    - **Expansion**: Increasing the money supply lowers the cost of borrowing, making loans cheaper for consumers and businesses.
    - **Contraction**: Reducing the money supply raises interest rates, increasing borrowing costs.
- **Inflation**: Inflation occurs when the money supply grows faster than the economy's output of goods and services.
    - **Demand-Pull**: Excess money in the hands of consumers increases demand, which "chases" limited goods and drives up prices.

  - **Hyperinflation**: If the gap between money growth and economic output becomes extreme, the currency's value can rapidly deteriorate.

- **Economic Growth (GDP)**: Adequate money supply is necessary to support production and trade.
  - **Short-run Stimulus**: Increased liquidity can boost investment and consumption, leading to higher GDP and lower unemployment.
  - **Long-run Neutrality**: Some economists argue that while money affects output in the short term, its long-term effect is primarily on price levels rather than real productivity (money neutrality).

## 2. Mechanisms of Economic Impact

- **Consumer Spending**: Lower interest rates from a high money supply encourage spending on big-ticket items like homes and cars.
- **Business Investment**: Cheap credit allows firms to expand, order more raw materials, and increase production capacity.
- **The Circular Flow**: Money acts as the "blood" of the economy, moving between households (labor providers) and businesses (producers) through wages and consumption.
- **Asset Prices**: High liquidity can lead to rising stock market prices and the potential formation of asset bubbles.

## 3. Monetary Policy Tools

Central banks use specific instruments to regulate these effects:

- **Repo Rate**: The rate at which the central bank lends to commercial banks; raising it reduces the money supply.

- **Open Market Operations (OMOs)**: Buying government securities injects cash into the system, while selling them absorbs liquidity.
- **Reserve Requirements (CRR/SLR)**: Mandating that banks hold a portion of deposits as reserves limits the amount they can lend out.

## 4. Summary of Macroeconomic Relationships

| Factor | Effect of Increased Money Supply | Effect of Decreased Money Supply |
|---|---|---|
| **Interest Rates** | Decrease (cheaper borrowing) | Increase (costlier borrowing) |
| **Consumer Demand** | Increase (higher spending) | Decrease (lower spending) |
| **Investment** | Increase (business expansion) | Decrease (delayed projects) |
| **Inflation** | Potential increase (rising prices) | Potential decrease (stable or falling prices) |
| **Unemployment** | Generally decreases (hiring grows) | Generally increases (production slows) |

## Key Takeaways

1. **Money supply and interest rates share an inverse relationship**

   More money means cheaper borrowing; less money means costlier credit.

2. **Inflation arises when money growth outpaces economic output**

   Demand-pull inflation and hyperinflation are the key risks of excessive money supply.

3. **GDP responds in the short run, but long-run effects are debated**

   Money neutrality suggests prices — not real productivity — are affected over time.

4. **Central banks use repo rates, OMOs, and reserve requirements to maintain balance**

   These tools allow the RBI to steer the economy between growth and stability.

CHAPTER 4 SUMMARY

# Macroeconomic Relationships at a Glance

The table below summarises how **increasing** or **decreasing** the money supply affects key economic factors.

| Factor | Increased Money Supply | Decreased Money Supply |
|---|---|---|
| Interest Rates | Decrease (cheaper borrowing) | Increase (costlier borrowing) |
| Consumer Demand | Increase (higher spending) | Decrease (lower spending) |
| Investment | Increase (business expansion) | Decrease (delayed projects) |
| Inflation | Potential increase (rising prices) | Potential decrease (stable/falling prices) |
| Unemployment | Generally decreases (hiring grows) | Generally increases (production slows) |

CHAPTER 3 MONETARY POLICY TOOLS

# How Central Banks Regulate the Economy

Central banks use specific instruments to control the money supply and steer the economy. These tools allow them to respond to changing conditions — injecting liquidity during slowdowns and absorbing it during overheating.

### Repo Rate

The rate at which the central bank lends to commercial banks. **Raising it reduces** the money supply; lowering it expands it.

### Open Market Operations

**Buying** government securities injects cash into the system, while **selling** them absorbs liquidity from circulation.

### Reserve Requirements (CRR/SLR)

Mandating that banks hold a portion of deposits as reserves **limits the amount** they can lend out to the public.

## The Circular Flow in Action

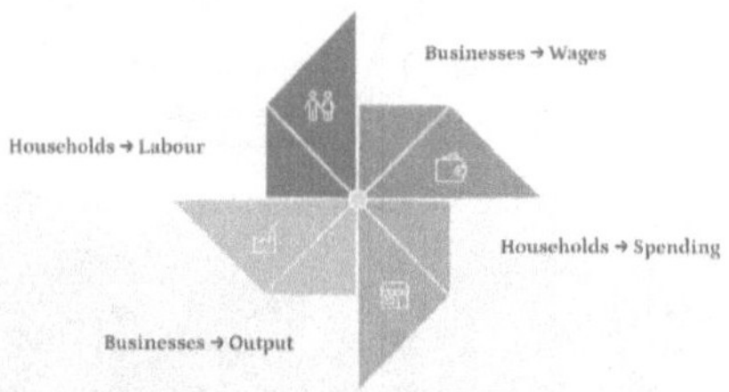


This continuous cycle of income and expenditure is what keeps the economy alive. When money supply increases, this flow accelerates — boosting both production and consumption simultaneously.

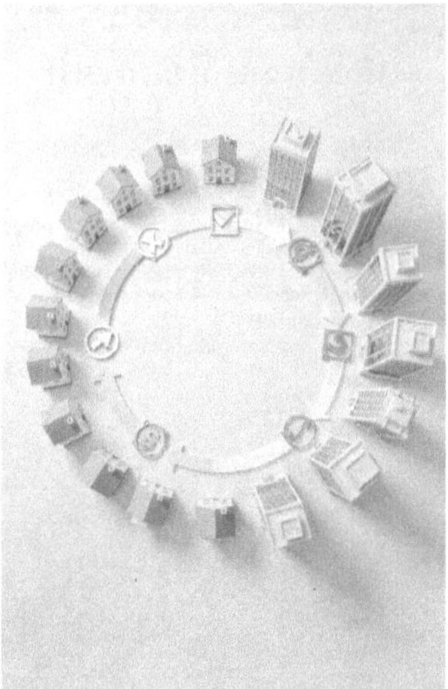

CHAPTER 2 MECHANISMS OF IMPACT

# How Money Moves Through the Economy

Money acts as the **"blood" of the economy**, flowing between households and businesses through wages and consumption. Here are the key mechanisms through which money supply changes translate into real economic effects.

### Consumer Spending

Lower interest rates encourage spending on big-ticket items like **homes and cars**.

### Business Investment

Cheap credit allows firms to **expand, order raw materials,** and increase production capacity.

### The Circular Flow

Money moves between households (labour providers) and businesses (producers) through **wages and consumption**.

### Asset Prices

High liquidity can lead to **rising stock prices** and the potential formation of **asset bubbles**.

# Economic Growth (GDP): Short-Run vs Long-Run

Adequate money supply is necessary to support production and trade — but its effects differ across time horizons.

### Short-Run Stimulus

Increased liquidity boosts investment and consumption, leading to **higher GDP** and **lower unemployment**.

### Long-Run Neutrality

Some economists argue money's long-term effect is primarily on **price levels** rather than real productivity — known as **money neutrality**.

## Inflation: When Money Outpaces Output

Inflation occurs when the money supply grows **faster than the economy's output** of goods and services. The consequences range from mild price increases to devastating currency collapse.

### Demand-Pull Inflation

Excess money in consumers' hands increases demand, which "chases" limited goods and **drives up prices** across the economy.

### Hyperinflation

When the gap between money growth and economic output becomes extreme, the currency's value can **rapidly deteriorate**, eroding savings and destabilising society.

## Interest Rates: The Inverse Relationship

There is an **inverse relationship** between money supply and interest rates — one of the most fundamental dynamics in economics.

### Expansion

Increasing the money supply **lowers borrowing costs**, making loans cheaper for consumers and businesses alike.

### Contraction

Reducing the money supply **raises interest rates**, increasing the cost of borrowing and cooling economic activity.

CHAPTER 1 KEY ECONOMIC INDICATORS

## How Money Supply Influences the Economy

The total amount of money available in an economy — the **money supply** — has a profound impact on macroeconomic variables. Central banks like the **Reserve Bank of India (RBI)** carefully manage this supply to balance stimulating development with preventing economic overheating.

Three critical indicators respond directly to changes in money supply: **interest rates, inflation,** and **GDP growth**. Understanding these relationships is essential to grasping how monetary decisions ripple through every corner of the economy.

## The Effect of Money on the Economy

Understanding how money supply shapes inflation, interest rates, growth, and the tools central banks use to keep the balance.

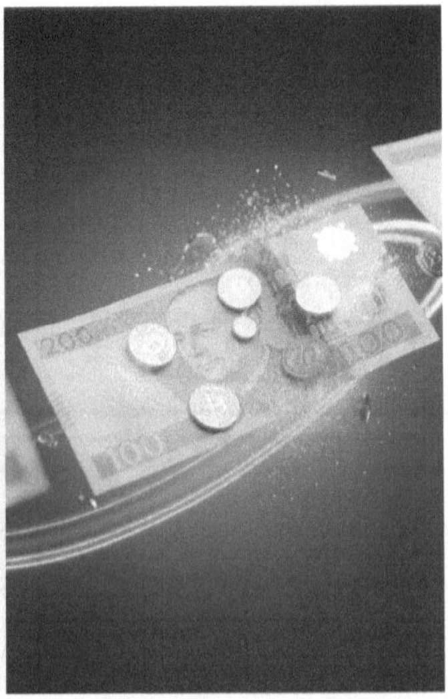

# 08

# Money Versus Asset, Which is Better

The choice between holding **Money** (cash) and **Assets** (investments) depends on your immediate needs versus long-term goals. While cash provides security and speed, assets are necessary for building wealth.

## Core Comparison

- **Money** is a medium of exchange used for immediate transactions and short-term stability.
- **Assets** (such as stocks, real estate, or gold) are resources intended to generate future income or appreciate in value.

| **Feature** | **Money (Cash)** | **Assets (Investments)** |
|---|---|---|
| **Primary Goal** | Liquidity & Safety | Wealth Growth & Income |
| **Inflation** | Value is eroded over time | Often acts as a hedge against inflation |
| **Risk** | Low nominal risk, high purchasing power risk | Market volatility and potential for loss |
| **Returns** | Minimal to none | Potential for high compounding returns |

## When Money is Better

Holding cash or cash equivalents (like savings accounts or Money Market Funds) is superior for:

- **Emergency Funds**: Maintaining 3–6 months of expenses for unexpected events.
- **Short-term Needs**: Funding purchases planned within the next 1–3 years.
- **Psychological Security**: Providing peace of mind during extreme market volatility.
- **Opportunity Capital**: Having "dry powder" ready to buy assets when market prices drop.

## When Assets are Better

Investing in assets is necessary for long-term financial success because:

- **Beating Inflation**: Over 30 years, equities have significantly outperformed traditional "safe" options like FDs.
- **Passive Income**: Assets like rental properties or dividend-paying stocks "make money while you sleep".
- **Compounding**: Assets allow your profits to earn more profits, leading to exponential growth.
- **Wealth Maximization**: While money is "spent," assets "build" your net worth sustainably.

## The Hybrid Approach

Most financial experts recommend a **balanced portfolio** rather than choosing one over the other:

- **The 70:20:10 Rule**: A common strategy allocates 70% to low-risk (often liquid) holdings, 20% to medium-risk, and 10% to high-risk assets.
- **Asset Allocation**: Spread wealth across different classes (equities, gold, bonds, and cash) to reduce overall risk.

# When to Hold Cash vs. When to Invest

### When Money is Better

Holding cash or equivalents like savings accounts or **Money Market Funds** is superior for:

- **Emergency Funds** — Maintain 3–6 months of expenses for unexpected events
- **Short-term Needs** — Purchases planned within 1–3 years
- **Psychological Security** — Peace of mind during extreme market volatility
- **Opportunity Capital** — "Dry powder" ready to buy assets when prices drop

### When Assets are Better

Investing in assets is necessary for long-term financial success because:

- **Beating Inflation** — Over 30 years, equities significantly outperform FDs
- **Passive Income** — Rental properties or dividend stocks "make money while you sleep"
- **Compounding** — Profits earn more profits, leading to exponential growth
- **Wealth Maximisation** — Money is "spent," but assets "build" net worth sustainably

THE HYBRID APPROACH

## A Balanced Portfolio Wins

Most financial experts recommend a **balanced portfolio** rather than choosing one over the other.

### The 70:20:10 Rule

Allocate 70% to low-risk (liquid) holdings, 20% to medium-risk, and 10% to high-risk assets.

### Asset Allocation

Spread wealth across equities, gold, bonds, and cash to reduce overall risk.

# Money vs. Assets: Where Should Your Wealth Live?

The choice between holding **Money** (cash) and **Assets** (investments) depends on your immediate needs versus long-term goals. While cash provides security and speed, assets are necessary for building wealth.

CORE COMPARISON

### Money

A medium of exchange used for immediate transactions and short-term stability.

### Assets

Resources like stocks, real estate, or gold intended to generate future income or appreciate in value.

| Feature | Money (Cash) | Assets (Investments) |
|---|---|---|
| Primary Goal | Liquidity & Safety | Wealth Growth & Income |
| Inflation | Value eroded over time | Often hedges against inflation |
| Risk | Low nominal risk, high purchasing power risk | Market volatility & potential for loss |
| Returns | Minimal to none | Potential for high compounding returns |

# 09

# Does Money Create Social Gap or Upliftment

Money plays a dual role in society, acting simultaneously as a primary driver of **social gaps** and a vital tool for **social upliftment**. Its impact is largely determined by how it is distributed and the quality of the institutional systems managing it.

## Money as a Driver of Social Gaps

The unequal distribution of money creates systemic barriers that entrench social stratification.

- **Unequal Opportunity**: Wealth provides superior access to high-quality education, healthcare, and professional networks, while those with less money face underfunded schools and limited services.
- **Reduced Social Mobility**: High income inequality is often linked to low social mobility, trapping families in a "cycle of poverty" where birth circumstances dictate future success.
- **Political Imbalance**: Significant wealth allows individuals and corporations to disproportionately influence public policy through lobbying and campaign financing, often at the expense of the general public.

- **Social Disconnection**: Economic gaps lead to physical and social segregation, such as the coexistence of luxury high-rises and slums, which can fuel social unrest and resentment.
- **Status Signalling**: Money acts as a status signal; its absence often leads to social exclusion and a loss of prestige, further widening the psychological gap between classes.

## Money as a Tool for Social Upliftment

When managed effectively, money is a powerful instrument for improving living standards and empowering individuals.

- **Financial Inclusion**: Providing access to banking, credit, and insurance allows marginalized populations to invest in businesses, manage risks, and save for the future.
- **Empowerment of Vulnerable Groups**: Targeted cash transfers, particularly to women, have shown to improve household well-being, child education, and food security.
- **Economic Specialization**: Money facilitates trade and allows individuals to specialize in skills, which enhances overall productivity and helps people move up the economic ladder.
- **Social Safety Nets**: Government redistribution through welfare and unemployment benefits provides a critical floor, preventing individuals from falling into absolute deprivation during crises.
- **Community Building**: In some contexts, money is used to strengthen social bonds through mutual support systems, such as family projects or community-based savings groups.

## Summary of Impacts

| Aspect | Money Creating Gaps | Money Driving Upliftment |
|---|---|---|
| **Education** | Quality education is reserved for the wealthy. | Funding/scholarships break the poverty loop. |
| **Politics** | Wealthy elites dominate policy decisions. | Financial inclusion empowers every voice. |
| **Social Life** | Segregation of "haves" and "have-nots". | Mutual assistance within supportive networks. |
| **Growth** | Inequality can depress overall economic growth. | Investment in individuals creates positive returns. |

CHAPTER 3 COMPARISON

# Summary of Impacts

The same resource — money — produces vastly different outcomes depending on how it flows through society. Here is a side-by-side view across key dimensions.

| Aspect | Money Creating Gaps | Money Driving Upliftment |
|---|---|---|
| **Education** | Quality education is reserved for the wealthy. | Funding and scholarships break the poverty loop. |
| **Politics** | Wealthy elites dominate policy decisions. | Financial inclusion empowers every voice. |
| **Social Life** | Segregation of "haves" and "have-nots". | Mutual assistance within supportive networks. |
| **Growth** | Inequality can depress overall economic growth. | Investment in individuals creates positive returns. |

# The Upliftment Pathway

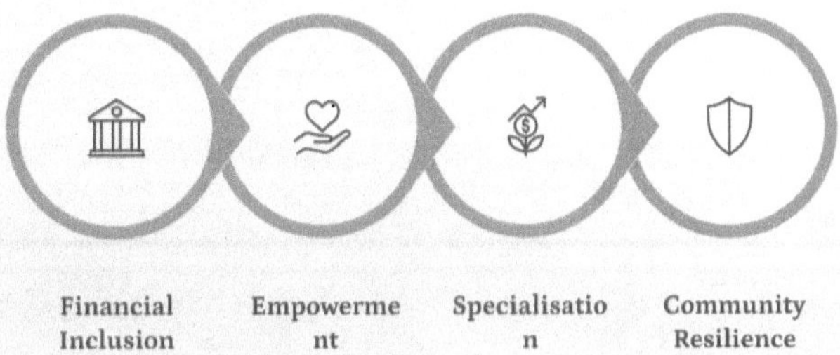


When channelled through inclusive institutions, money creates a virtuous cycle — from individual empowerment to collective prosperity.

## Specialisation, Safety Nets & Community

### Economic Specialisation

Money facilitates trade and allows individuals to specialise in skills, enhancing overall productivity and helping people move up the economic ladder.

### Social Safety Nets

Government redistribution through welfare and unemployment benefits provides a critical floor, preventing individuals from falling into absolute deprivation during crises.

### Community Building

Money strengthens social bonds through mutual support systems — family projects and community-based savings groups that uplift entire neighbourhoods together.

## Financial Inclusion & Empowerment

### Financial Inclusion

Providing access to banking, credit, and insurance allows marginalised populations to invest in businesses, manage risks, and save for the future — unlocking economic participation for millions.

### Empowerment of Vulnerable Groups

Targeted cash transfers, particularly to women, have shown to improve household well-being, child education, and food security. Direct financial support creates ripple effects across entire communities.

CHAPTER 2 THE UPLIFT

## Money as a Tool for Social Upliftment

When managed effectively, money is a powerful instrument for improving living standards and empowering individuals. The key lies in inclusive systems that channel resources to those who need them most.

## The Widening Gap at a Glance

Each of these factors reinforces the others, creating a self-perpetuating system where wealth begets wealth and poverty deepens across generations.

## Political Imbalance & Social Disconnection

### Political Imbalance

Significant wealth allows individuals and corporations to disproportionately influence public policy through lobbying and campaign financing — often at the expense of the general public.

### Social Disconnection

Economic gaps lead to physical and social segregation — luxury high-rises coexisting with slums — fuelling social unrest and deep resentment between communities.

### Status Signalling

Money acts as a status signal; its absence often leads to social exclusion and a loss of prestige, further widening the psychological gap between classes.

## Unequal Opportunity & Reduced Mobility

### Unequal Opportunity

Wealth provides superior access to high-quality education, healthcare, and professional networks. Those with less money face underfunded schools and limited services, creating a widening gap from the very start of life.

### Reduced Social Mobility

High income inequality is often linked to low social mobility, trapping families in a **"cycle of poverty"** where birth circumstances dictate future success. Escaping this cycle becomes exponentially harder with each generation.

## The Dual Role of Money in Society

Money acts simultaneously as a primary driver of **social gaps** and a vital tool for **social upliftment**. Its impact is largely determined by how it is distributed and the quality of the institutional systems managing it.

## The Path Forward

Money's impact is not predetermined — it is shaped by the systems, policies, and choices we make as a society.

**Distribute Equitably**

Close systemic gaps through inclusive policy.

**Empower Individuals**

Channel resources to those who need them most.

**Strengthen Institutions**

Build transparent systems that serve everyone.

# 10

# Principals of Money in Globalization and Global Climate Action

The principles of money in globalization and global climate action are increasingly defined by a shift from high-level commitments to **structural execution** and the **integration of climate risk** into the global financial architecture. As of early 2026, global finance is being "rewired" to address the multi-trillion-dollar gap required for a just transition.

## Core Principles of Global Climate Finance

1. **Common but Differentiated Responsibilities (CBDR)**: A foundational principle under the UNFCCC, requiring wealthier nations that historically emitted more to lead in providing financial and technical support to developing countries.
2. **Climate Justice & Equity**: Financial flows should be **predominantly grant-based** rather than loans for the most vulnerable nations to avoid exacerbating debt burdens.
3. **The "Polluter Pays" Principle**: Advocates for taxes on high-emission industries, such as fossil fuel windfall profits or levies on private aviation, to generate new climate funds.
4. **Additionality**: Ensuring that climate finance is "new and additional" to existing Official Development Assistance (ODA), rather than simply re-labeling old aid.

5. **Mainstreaming**: Integrating climate considerations into the core lending and investment strategies of all financial institutions, treating climate as a **material financial risk** rather than an elective ESG metric.

## Money in a Globalized Climate Response

- **De-risking & Blended Finance**: To attract the necessary **$1.3 trillion annually** by 2035, public funds are increasingly used as "risk capital" (guarantees and first-loss tranches) to "crowd in" private investment for high-risk, low-carbon projects in emerging markets.
- **Currency & Sovereign Risk**: The "hierarchy of currencies" forces developing nations to borrow in hard currencies (USD/EUR), exposing them to high interest rates and exchange rate volatility that can make green infrastructure projects economically unviable.
- **Market-Based Mechanisms**: The operationalization of **Article 6** of the Paris Agreement is driving the growth of high-integrity carbon markets, allowing for the discovery of carbon prices to incentivize global decarbonization.
- **South-South Cooperation**: Emerging economies (notably the **BRICS** group) are increasingly using their own multilateral banks and local currency financing to reduce dependence on Western-dominated financial systems.

## Emerging Financial Trends (2026)

- **Prudential Regulation**: Central banks are moving from voluntary guidance to **enforcement**, requiring banks to hold capital buffers against climate shocks and integrating climate-related "stress tests" into financial stability assessments.

- **Loss & Damage Fund**: Focus has shifted to the rapid capitalization and disbursement of funds to help climate-vulnerable communities recover from unavoidable disasters.
- **Nature-Positive Finance**: Growing recognition that climate and biodiversity are linked; finance is shifting toward **nature-based solutions** and assessing "nature-related financial disclosures".

## Key Takeaways

1 **Principles Matter**

CBDR, climate justice, polluter pays, additionality, and mainstreaming form the ethical and structural backbone of climate finance.

2 **Scale Demands Innovation**

Blended finance, carbon markets, and South-South cooperation are essential to mobilise **$1.3 trillion annually** by 2035.

3 **Regulation Is Accelerating**

Central banks, loss & damage funds, and nature-positive disclosures are moving climate from voluntary pledges to **mandatory financial infrastructure**.

## The Full Picture: Climate Finance Architecture

The architecture of global climate finance weaves together foundational principles, innovative instruments, and emerging regulatory frameworks into a coherent system designed to close the funding gap.

## Loss & Damage and Nature-Positive Finance

**Loss & Damage Fund**

Focus has shifted to **rapid capitalisation and disbursement** of funds to help climate-vulnerable communities recover from unavoidable disasters — moving from pledges to action.

**Nature-Positive Finance**

Growing recognition that climate and biodiversity are linked. Finance is shifting toward **nature-based solutions** and assessing "nature-related financial disclosures".

## Prudential Regulation & Climate Stress Tests

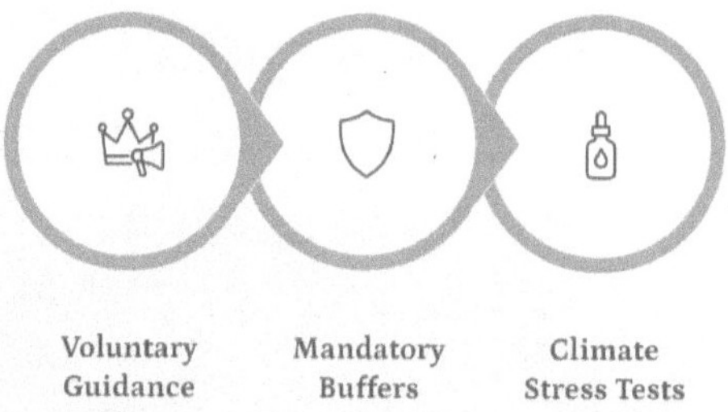


Central banks are moving from voluntary guidance to **enforcement**, requiring banks to hold capital buffers against climate shocks and integrating climate-related stress tests into financial stability assessments.

CHAPTER 3

# Emerging Financial Trends — 2026

Three powerful shifts are reshaping the frontier of climate finance: prudential regulation, loss and damage funding, and nature-positive investment.

## Currency Risk & Market Mechanisms

### Currency & Sovereign Risk

The "hierarchy of currencies" forces developing nations to borrow in hard currencies (USD/EUR), exposing them to **high interest rates and exchange rate volatility** that can render green projects unviable.

### Market-Based Mechanisms

Operationalisation of **Article 6 of the Paris Agreement** is driving high-integrity carbon markets, enabling carbon price discovery to incentivise global decarbonisation.

## De-risking & Blended Finance

To attract the necessary **$1.3 trillion annually by 2035**, public funds are increasingly deployed as "risk capital" — guarantees and first-loss tranches — to **"crowd in" private investment** for high-risk, low-carbon projects in emerging markets.

This blended finance approach transforms the risk-return profile of green infrastructure, making projects bankable that would otherwise never attract institutional capital.

**$1.3T**

Annual Target

Required by 2035 for climate action

CHAPTER 2

## Money in a Globalised Climate Response

Mobilising capital at the scale required demands innovative financial instruments, risk-sharing mechanisms, and a rethinking of how currencies and markets shape climate outcomes.

## Polluter Pays, Additionality & Mainstreaming

**1**

### Polluter Pays Principle

Advocates for taxes on high-emission industries — fossil fuel windfall profits, levies on private aviation — to generate **new climate funds**.

**2**

### Additionality

Climate finance must be **"new and additional"** to existing Official Development Assistance (ODA), not simply re-labelled old aid commitments.

**3**

### Mainstreaming

Integrating climate considerations into the **core lending and investment strategies** of all financial institutions, treating climate as a material financial risk.

## CBDR & Climate Justice

### Common but Differentiated Responsibilities

A foundational UNFCCC principle requiring **wealthier nations** that historically emitted more to lead in providing financial and technical support to developing countries.

### Climate Justice & Equity

Financial flows should be predominantly **grant-based rather than loans** for the most vulnerable nations — avoiding the trap of exacerbating existing debt burdens.

CHAPTER 1

# Core Principles of Global Climate Finance

Five foundational principles now govern how climate money flows across borders — shaping who pays, who receives, and on what terms.

OVERVIEW

## The Landscape of Climate Finance in 2026

As of early 2026, global finance is undergoing a fundamental rewiring. The era of high-level pledges is giving way to **structural execution** — integrating climate risk directly into the global financial architecture.

The challenge is immense: bridging a multi-trillion-dollar funding gap to enable a **just transition** that leaves no nation behind. This demands new principles, innovative instruments, and a reimagined relationship between public and private capital.

**Key Shift**

From voluntary commitments to mandatory integration of climate as a **material financial risk** — not an elective ESG metric.

# Money, Globalisation & Global Climate Action

How global finance is being rewired to close the multi-trillion-dollar gap for a just transition — from high-level commitments to structural execution.

# 11

# What is Decentralize Financing

Decentralised Finance (DeFi) is an emerging, blockchain-based financial ecosystem that replicates traditional financial services—such as lending, borrowing, and trading—without the need for central intermediaries like banks, brokers, or exchanges.

## 1. Core Infrastructure and Mechanics

DeFi operates through a layered technical stack that replaces human oversight with automated code.

- **Blockchain Networks**: Serves as the underlying immutable ledger. While Ethereum is the dominant platform, others like Solana and Binance Smart Chain are widely used.
- **Smart Contracts**: Self-executing programs that automatically enforce the terms of a financial agreement when predetermined conditions are met.
- **Decentralised Apps (dApps)**: User interfaces that allow individuals to interact with these smart contracts using digital wallets (e.g., MetaMask).
- **Oracles**: Services like Chainlink that bridge off-chain data (e.g., real-world asset prices) to the blockchain to trigger smart contracts.

## 2. Primary Financial Services

DeFi applications cover nearly every function found in traditional "Wall Street" finance:

- **Decentralised Exchanges (DEXs)**: Platforms like Uniswap allow peer-to-peer trading via "Automated Market Makers" (AMMs) rather than centralized order books.
- **Lending and Borrowing**: Protocols like Aave and compound let users earn interest by lending assets or borrow against overcollateralized crypto holdings.
- **Stablecoins**: Digital assets pegged to fiat currencies (e.g., DAI, USDC) to provide price stability within the volatile crypto market.
- **Yield Farming & Staking**: Strategies where users provide liquidity or lock assets to secure a network in exchange for rewards and passive income.
- **Derivatives & Synthetics**: Creation of synthetic assets that track the value of real-world stocks, commodities, or indices.

## 3. Comparative Analysis: DeFi vs. Traditional Finance (TradFi)

| Feature | Traditional Finance (TradFi) | Decentralised Finance (DeFi) |
|---|---|---|
| **Control** | Centralized (Banks/ Governments) | Distributed (Users/Code) |
| **Access** | Permissioned (KYC/ Identity checks) | Permissionless (Anyone with a wallet) |
| **Transparency** | Opaque (Private records) | Fully Transparent (Public ledger) |

| Feature | Traditional Finance (TradFi) | Decentralised Finance (DeFi) |
|---|---|---|
| **Speed** | Manual (Days for settlement) | Instant (Seconds/ Minutes) |
| **Custody** | Institutional (Banks hold assets) | Self-Custodial (Users hold keys) |

## 4. Critical Risks and Challenges

Despite its growth, DeFi is currently in an experimental phase and carries substantial risks:

- **Smart Contract Vulnerabilities**: Errors or "bugs" in code can be exploited by hackers, often leading to irreversible loss of funds.
- **Market Volatility**: Extreme price fluctuations can trigger automated liquidations of collateralized positions.
- **Regulatory Uncertainty**: Global regulators (e.g., SEC) are still developing frameworks to address AML (Anti-Money Laundering) and investor protection in decentralized settings.
- **Complexity & UX**: High technical barriers and unintuitive user interfaces make it difficult for average retail users to navigate safely.
- **Scams**: The lack of gatekeepers makes the space prone to "rug pulls" where developers abandon projects after attracting investor funds.

## Key Takeaways

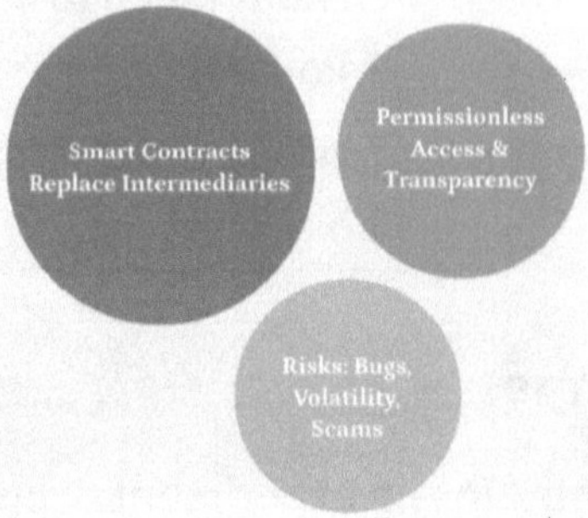


DeFi represents a paradigm shift in financial services—offering unprecedented access and transparency, but demanding caution, education, and awareness of its experimental nature before participation.

## The Risk Landscape

### Smart Contract Vulnerabilities

Errors or "bugs" in code can be exploited by hackers, often leading to **irreversible loss of funds**.

### Market Volatility

Extreme price fluctuations can trigger **automated liquidations** of collateralised positions.

### Regulatory Uncertainty

Global regulators (e.g., SEC) are still developing frameworks for **AML** and investor protection in decentralised settings.

### Complexity & UX

High technical barriers and unintuitive interfaces make it difficult for average retail users to navigate safely.

### Scams & Rug Pulls

The lack of gatekeepers makes the space prone to developers abandoning projects after attracting investor funds.

CHAPTER 4

## Critical Risks & Challenges

Despite its growth, DeFi is currently in an **experimental phase** and carries substantial risks that every participant must understand before engaging.

CHAPTER 3

## DeFi vs. Traditional Finance

A head-to-head comparison across the dimensions that matter most to users, regulators, and institutions.

| **Feature** | **Traditional Finance (TradFi)** | **Decentralised Finance (DeFi)** |
|---|---|---|
| Control | Centralised (Banks/Governments) | Distributed (Users/Code) |
| Access | Permissioned (KYC/Identity checks) | Permissionless (Anyone with a wallet) |
| Transparency | Opaque (Private records) | Fully Transparent (Public ledger) |
| Speed | Manual (Days for settlement) | Instant (Seconds/Minutes) |
| Custody | Institutional (Banks hold assets) | Self-Custodial (Users hold keys) |

## Stablecoins, Yield & Synthetics

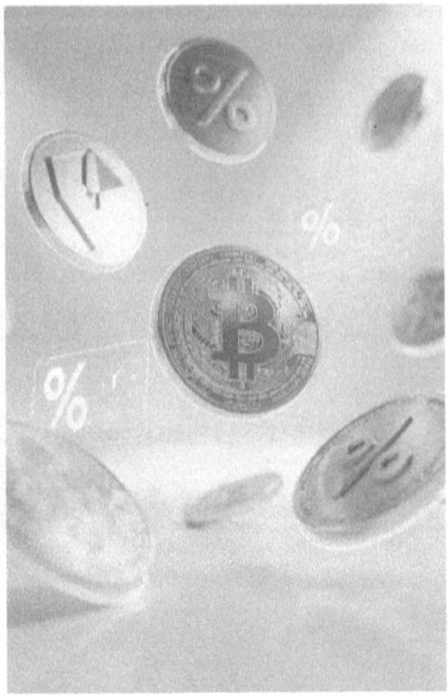

### Stablecoins

Digital assets pegged to fiat currencies (e.g., **DAI, USDC**) providing price stability within the volatile crypto market.

### Yield Farming & Staking

Users provide liquidity or lock assets to secure a network in exchange for rewards and passive income.

### Derivatives & Synthetics

Creation of synthetic assets that track the value of real-world stocks, commodities, or indices on-chain.

## Trading & Lending in DeFi

### Decentralised Exchanges (DEXs)

Platforms like **Uniswap** allow peer-to-peer trading via **Automated Market Makers (AMMs)** rather than centralised order books. Users trade directly from their wallets.

### Lending & Borrowing

Protocols like **Aave** and **Compound** let users earn interest by lending assets or borrow against overcollateralised crypto holdings—all without a bank.

CHAPTER 2

# Primary Financial Services

DeFi applications cover nearly every function found in traditional "Wall Street" finance—from trading and lending to derivatives and passive income strategies.

## The DeFi Technology Stack

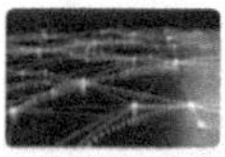

### Blockchain Networks

The underlying immutable ledger. While **Ethereum** is the dominant platform, others like **Solana** and **Binance Smart Chain** are widely used.

### Smart Contracts

Self-executing programs that automatically enforce the terms of a financial agreement when predetermined conditions are met.

### dApps & Wallets

User interfaces allowing individuals to interact with smart contracts using digital wallets like **MetaMask**.

### Oracles

Services like **Chainlink** that bridge off-chain data (e.g., real-world asset prices) to the blockchain to trigger smart contracts.

CHAPTER 1

# Core Infrastructure & Mechanics

DeFi operates through a layered technical stack that replaces human oversight with automated code. Each layer serves a distinct purpose in enabling trustless, permissionless financial services.

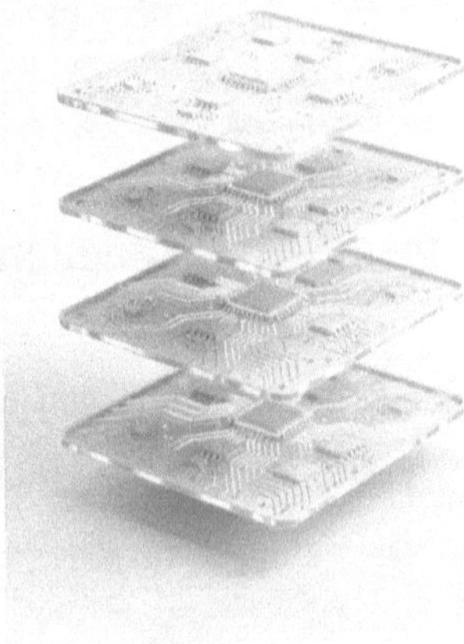

OVERVIEW

## What We'll Cover

A structured journey through the DeFi landscape—from foundational technology to real-world applications and the risks that come with this financial revolution.

01

### Core Infrastructure

The technical stack powering DeFi

02

### Financial Services

DEXs, lending, stablecoins & more

03

### DeFi vs. TradFi

A head-to-head comparison

04

### Risks & Challenges

What every participant must know

## Decentralised Finance (DeFi)

An emerging, blockchain-based financial ecosystem that replicates traditional financial services—such as lending, borrowing, and trading—without the need for central intermediaries like banks, brokers, or exchanges.

# 12

# Is Cryptocurrency is the Future

As of 2026, cryptocurrency is no longer viewed merely as a speculative niche but is maturing into a **permanent layer of global financial infrastructure**. While it is unlikely to entirely replace traditional fiat currencies in the near term, it is increasingly operating as a "parallel financial system" that integrates with traditional banking, payments, and corporate treasuries.

## 1. Institutional Integration & "Digital Gold"

- **Strategic Reserve Asset**: Bitcoin has transitioned from a trading product to a legitimate treasury asset.
- By 2026, public companies and even some sovereign nations are treating Bitcoin as operational capital.
    - The U.S. established a **Strategic Bitcoin Reserve** in 2025, further legitimizing its role as a store of value.
    - **Institutional Inflows**: The success of spot Bitcoin and Ethereum ETFs has created a stable, regulated channel for institutional capital, which now accounts for roughly **24.5% of Bitcoin ETF holdings**.

## 2. The Rise of "Internet Dollars" (Stablecoins)

- **Settlement Backbone**: Stablecoins (like USDC and USDT) have become the "quiet workhorse" of global payments.
- **Real-World Utility**: They are increasingly used for cross-border B2B payments, global payroll, and remittances, often settling in seconds at a fraction of traditional banking costs.
- **Corporate Adoption**: Approximately **34% of small and medium businesses (SMBs)** now use crypto for operations, a significant increase from previous years.

## 3. Tokenization of Real-World Assets (RWA)

- **Mainstream Shift**: Moving beyond pilots, financial giants like BlackRock, JPMorgan, and Goldman Sachs are actively tokenizing traditional assets such as U.S. Treasuries, private credit, and real estate.
- **Efficiency Gains**: Tokenization allows for fractional ownership and 24/7 trading of otherwise illiquid assets, potentially growing into a **multi-trillion dollar market by 2030**.

## 4. Evolving Regulatory Landscape

- **From Risk to Catalyst**: Clearer frameworks like the **GENIUS Act** in the U.S. and **MiCA** in the EU are providing the legal certainty necessary for banks to offer crypto services.
- **Mandatory Oversight**: Regulation is shifting from voluntary to mandatory, with major hubs like Hong Kong and Singapore establishing formal licensing regimes.

## 5. Key Challenges to Future Dominance

- **Volatility**: High price swings remain a barrier for everyday retail use as a standard medium of exchange.
- **Complexity**: Technical hurdles like wallet management and private key security still deter non-technical users.
- **Environmental Concerns**: The high energy consumption of Proof-of-Work mining (e.g., Bitcoin) remains a subject of intense debate and a target for ESG-focused regulation.

## Summary Table: Future Outlook

| Feature | 2026 Status | Long-term Role |
|---|---|---|
| **Bitcoin** | Institutional store of value | "Digital Gold" / Reserve Asset |
| **Ethereum** | Network for DeFi and RWAs | Global Settlement Layer |
| **Stablecoins** | Emerging as "Internet Dollars" | Backbone of digital payments |
| **DeFi** | Professionalized infrastructure | Modular, automated banking |

# The Road Ahead

> Crypto is no longer asking for permission — it is building the parallel financial system of the future.

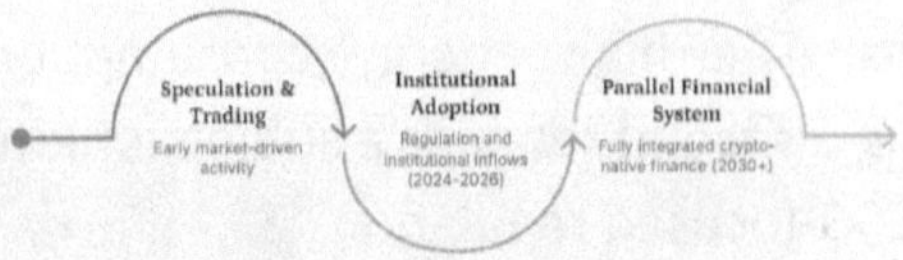


From Bitcoin as digital gold, to stablecoins as internet dollars, to tokenised real-world assets — the crypto ecosystem is maturing into a permanent, integrated layer of global finance.

# Future Outlook: Where Each Layer Is Headed

The crypto ecosystem is stratifying into distinct layers, each with a clear role in the financial system of tomorrow.

| Feature | 2026 Status | Long-term Role |
|---|---|---|
| **Bitcoin** | Institutional store of value | "Digital Gold" / Reserve Asset |
| **Ethereum** | Network for DeFi and RWAs | Global Settlement Layer |
| **Stablecoins** | Emerging as "Internet Dollars" | Backbone of digital payments |
| **DeFi** | Professionalised infrastructure | Modular, automated banking |

## Barriers That Remain

Despite rapid maturation, significant challenges still stand between crypto and mainstream dominance as an everyday financial tool.

### Volatility

High price swings remain a barrier for everyday retail use as a standard medium of exchange

### Complexity

Technical hurdles like wallet management and private key security still deter non-technical users

### Environmental Concerns

High energy consumption of Proof-of-Work mining (e.g., Bitcoin) remains a target for ESG-focused regulation

CHAPTER 5

# Key Challenges to Future Dominance

## From Risk to Catalyst

Regulation is shifting from voluntary to **mandatory**, providing the legal certainty necessary for banks to offer crypto services. Clearer frameworks are transforming regulation from a barrier into a growth catalyst.

### GENIUS Act (U.S.)

Providing comprehensive legal clarity for stablecoin issuance and crypto banking services

### MiCA (EU)

Europe's Markets in Crypto-Assets regulation establishing unified rules across member states

### Asia-Pacific Hubs

Hong Kong and Singapore establishing formal licensing regimes for crypto exchanges and services

CHAPTER 4

# Evolving Regulatory Landscape

## From Pilots to Mainstream

Moving beyond pilots, financial giants like **BlackRock, JPMorgan, and Goldman Sachs** are actively tokenising traditional assets such as U.S. Treasuries, private credit, and real estate.

### Fractional Ownership

Tokenisation enables investors to own fractions of otherwise illiquid assets

### 24/7 Trading

Assets can be traded around the clock, removing traditional market hour constraints

### Multi-Trillion Dollar Market

Potentially growing into a multi-trillion dollar market by 2030

**Assets Being Tokenised**

- U.S. Treasuries
- Private Credit
- Real Estate
- Commodities

CHAPTER 3

# Tokenisation of Real-World Assets

## Stablecoins: The Quiet Workhorse

Stablecoins like **USDC and USDT** have become the "quiet workhorse" of global payments — the settlement backbone of a new digital economy.

### Real-World Utility

Used for cross-border B2B payments, global payroll, and remittances — settling in seconds at a fraction of traditional banking costs.

### Corporate Adoption

Approximately **34% of SMBs** now use crypto for operations, a significant increase from previous years.

### Settlement Backbone

Stablecoins are emerging as the "Internet Dollars" powering the backbone of digital payments globally.

CHAPTER 2

# The Rise of "Internet Dollars"

## Bitcoin as a Strategic Reserve Asset

Bitcoin has transitioned from a trading product to a **legitimate treasury asset**. By 2026, public companies and even some sovereign nations are treating Bitcoin as operational capital.

### U.S. Strategic Bitcoin Reserve

Established in 2025, further legitimising Bitcoin's role as a store of value

### Institutional Inflows

Spot Bitcoin and Ethereum ETFs created stable, regulated channels for institutional capital

### Bitcoin ETF Holdings

Share now held by institutional investors

## The Landscape Has Shifted

As of 2026, cryptocurrency is no longer viewed merely as a speculative niche but is maturing into a permanent layer of global financial infrastructure. While it is unlikely to entirely replace traditional fiat currencies in the near term, it is increasingly operating as a **"parallel financial system"** that integrates with traditional banking, payments, and corporate treasuries.

### Speculation Era

Early crypto as a trading-only asset

### Institutional Adoption

ETFs, reserves, and corporate treasuries

### Parallel Financial System

Integrated with global banking and payments

# The Future of Cryptocurrency in 2026

From speculative niche to a permanent layer of global financial infrastructure — how crypto is becoming a parallel financial system.

# 13

# Concept of Money With Respect to Artificial Intelligence in Labour Market

The integration of Artificial Intelligence (AI) into the labour market is fundamentally altering the "concept of money" by shifting how value is generated, distributed, and captured between human labour and automated capital.

## 1. Shift from Labor to Capital Income

AI is driving a significant redistribution of national income, moving the "surplus" away from workers and toward the owners of technology.

- **Declining Labor Share**: Empirical studies show that industries adopting AI often see a 0.5 to 1.6 percentage point reduction in the labor share of income.
- **Capital-Biased Innovation**: Unlike previous waves of automation, AI acts as a capital-biased innovation, where returns from productivity gains increasingly accrue to the owners of algorithms, data, and patents rather than the workforce.
- **Concentration of Wealth**: This shift risks creating "superstar firms" that capture the majority of market profits, leading to greater economic inequality between firm owners and the broader labor force.

## 2. Wage Polarization and the "AI Premium"

The monetary value of human work is bifurcating based on whether a role complements or competes with AI.

- **The Skill Premium**: Workers with AI-related skills command a significant wage premium, recently estimated at **56%**.
- **Skill Compression**: High- and medium-skill occupations (e.g., law, finance) are experiencing "wage compression" as AI replicates cognitive tasks previously immune to automation.
- **Low-Skill Divergence**: While some low-skill service jobs remain stable due to the need for physical presence, entry-level roles face increased competition, further adjusting traditional wage structures.

## 3. Devaluation of Routine Cognitive Labor

Money, as a reward for labor, is increasingly tied to "bottleneck" tasks that machines cannot yet perform.

- **Efficiency vs. Price**: As AI makes cognitive tasks (like coding or data analysis) extremely cheap to produce, the market price of these services drops toward zero.
- **The "Bottleneck" Economy**: Economic value is shifting toward non-automatable human attributes such as empathy, complex problem-solving, and strategy.
- **Redefining "Work"**: Proponents of Universal Basic Income (UBI) argue for decoupling human value from traditional employment, proposing a "citizen's dividend" as a share of the collective wealth generated by AI.

## 4. Monetary Policy and Market Stability

AI's impact on the labor market also influences how money moves through the broader economy.

- **Algorithmic Pricing**: AI enables faster, flexible price adjustments by firms, which can amplify inflation shocks and challenge central bank management.
- **Consumption Patterns**: Shifts in wealth distribution affect the "marginal propensity to consume," altering how demand responds to interest rate changes or other monetary policy actions.

## 5. Emerging Monetary Safety Nets

The potential for large-scale displacement has led to serious proposals for new financial structures:

- **Robot/Automation Taxes**: Taxing companies that replace human workers with AI to fund social safety nets.
- **Universal Basic Income (UBI)**: Regular, unconditional cash payments to provide stability as traditional jobs become less reliable.

## Key Takeaways

1 **Income is shifting from labour to capital**

AI-adopting industries see a 0.5–1.6% decline in labour share, concentrating wealth among technology owners.

2 **Wages are polarising around AI fluency**

A 56% wage premium for AI skills, while routine cognitive roles face compression and devaluation.

3 **Value is migrating to human "bottlenecks"**

Empathy, strategy, and complex problem-solving define the new frontier of irreplaceable human worth.

4 **New safety nets are urgently needed**

Robot taxes and UBI proposals aim to redistribute AI-generated wealth and sustain economic stability.

## The Big Picture

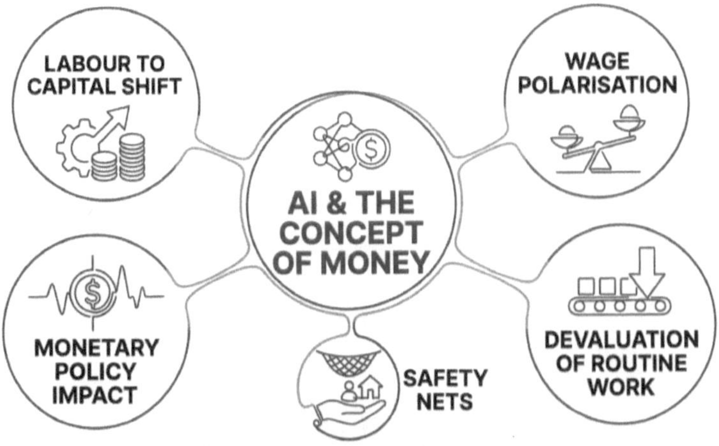


AI is not merely automating tasks — it is fundamentally rewriting the rules of how value is created, who captures it, and what money means in a world where machines increasingly do the work.

CHAPTER 5

# Emerging Monetary Safety Nets

The potential for large-scale displacement has led to serious proposals for new financial structures to protect workers and sustain economies.

### Robot / Automation Taxes

Taxing companies that replace human workers with AI to fund social safety nets — redirecting a portion of capital gains back into public welfare.

### Universal Basic Income (UBI)

Regular, unconditional cash payments to provide stability as traditional jobs become less reliable — a "citizen's dividend" from AI-generated wealth.

CHAPTER 4

# Monetary Policy & Market Stability

AI's impact on the labour market also influences how money moves through the broader economy, challenging traditional macroeconomic management.

### Algorithmic Pricing

AI enables faster, flexible price adjustments by firms, which can **amplify inflation shocks** and challenge central bank management of price stability.

### Consumption Patterns

Shifts in wealth distribution affect the **"marginal propensity to consume,"** altering how demand responds to interest rate changes or other monetary policy actions.

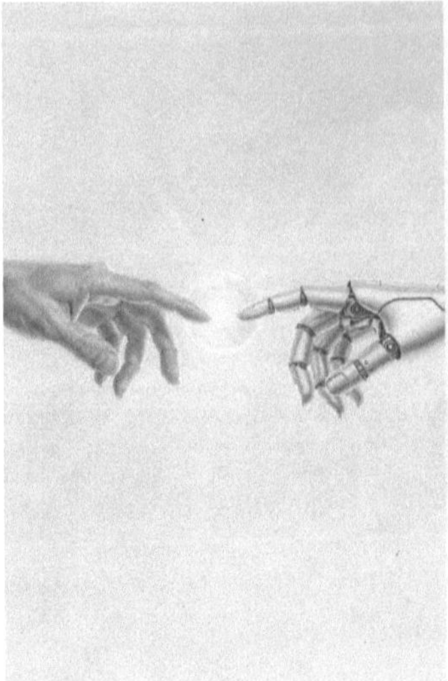

## Redefining "Work" Itself

Economic value is shifting toward **non-automatable human attributes** — empathy, complex problem-solving, and strategic thinking. These "bottleneck" capabilities define the new frontier of valuable labour.

Proponents of Universal Basic Income (UBI) argue for **decoupling human value from traditional employment**, proposing a "citizen's dividend" as a share of the collective wealth generated by AI.

### The Core Question

If machines can do the work, how do we define human worth — and who receives the monetary rewards?

CHAPTER 3

# Devaluation of Routine Cognitive Labour

Money, as a reward for labour, is increasingly tied to **"bottleneck" tasks** that machines cannot yet perform. As AI makes cognitive tasks like coding or data analysis extremely cheap to produce, the market price of these services drops toward zero.

### AI Efficiency

Cognitive tasks become near-zero cost to produce

### Price Collapse

Market price of routine services plummets

### Bottleneck Economy

Value shifts to empathy, strategy, and complex problem-solving

# Who Wins, Who Loses?

### The Skill Premium

Workers with AI-related skills command a wage premium recently estimated at **56%**. Demand for AI fluency is reshaping compensation structures across industries.

### Skill Compression

High- and medium-skill occupations (e.g., law, finance) experience **"wage compression"** as AI replicates cognitive tasks previously immune to automation.

### Low-Skill Divergence

Some low-skill service jobs remain stable due to physical presence needs, but entry-level roles face increased competition, further adjusting traditional wage structures.

CHAPTER 2

# Wage Polarisation & the "AI Premium"

The monetary value of human work is bifurcating based on whether a role **complements** or **competes** with AI. This creates a stark divide across the workforce.

## The Numbers Behind the Shift

**0.5–1.6%**

**Labour Share Decline**

Percentage point reduction in labour share of income in AI-adopting industries

**56%**

**AI Skill Premium**

Wage premium commanded by workers with AI-related skills

This shift risks creating **"superstar firms"** that capture the majority of market profits, leading to greater economic inequality between firm owners and the broader labour force. Concentration of wealth accelerates as capital-biased innovation compounds returns for technology owners.

CHAPTER 1

## Shift from Labour to Capital Income

AI is driving a significant redistribution of national income, moving the "surplus" away from workers and toward the owners of technology. Unlike previous waves of automation, AI acts as a **capital-biased innovation,** where returns from productivity gains increasingly accrue to the owners of algorithms, data, and patents rather than the workforce.

OVERVIEW

## What We'll Cover

01

**Labour to Capital Income**

The great redistribution of surplus

02

**Wage Polarisation**

The emerging "AI Premium"

03

**Devaluation of Routine Labour**

When cognitive work trends toward zero cost

04

**Monetary Policy & Stability**

How AI reshapes macroeconomic levers

05

**Emerging Safety Nets**

Robot taxes, UBI, and new financial structures

## AI & The Concept of Money

How Artificial Intelligence is fundamentally reshaping the way value is generated, distributed, and captured between human labour and automated capital.

# 14

# Concept of Money With Respect to Research in Space and Medical Technology

The concept of money in space and medical technology research is shifting from a traditional "cost" model to a "value creation" framework. Investments in these sectors are increasingly viewed as economic catalysts rather than mere expenditures, with a significant "multiplier effect" on terrestrial industries.

## 1. Economic Multiplier & Return on Investment (ROI)

Space and medical R&D generate substantial financial returns by spinning off technologies into commercial markets.

- **ISRO (India):** Estimated return of **2.54 times** every rupee spent, contributing approximately $60 billion to the national economy over the last decade.
- **NASA (USA):** Historical ROI estimates range from **$7 for every $1** spent during the Apollo era to as high as **$40 for every $1** in modern space development.
- **Sector Growth:** The space medicine market alone is projected to grow from $1.18 billion in 2024 to **$2.14 billion by 2029** (12.5% CAGR).

## 2. The "Space Value of Money" (SVoM)

A new financial principle, the **Space Value of Money**, suggests that space should be integrated as a foundational dimension of value in finance.

- **Monetisation of Space:** Proposes creating money based on space-based value creation, using new instruments like **Public Capitalisation Notes (PCNs)** for central bank funding.
- **Space Currency:** Concepts like the **"Quid"** have been designed to withstand space travel stresses, anticipating a future where electronic transfers are disrupted by astronomical distances.
- **Cis-lunar Economy:** The first phase of this economy will likely be based on **in-situ resource utilization (ISRU)**, using lunar water and oxygen to support activity rather than shipping resources from Earth.

## 3. Medical Spinoffs as Commercial Assets

Medical technologies developed for extreme space conditions often become multi-billion dollar terrestrial industries.

- **Diagnostic Imaging:** Digital image processing originally used for moon landing photos directly led to the development of **MRI and CT scans.**
- **Vision Correction:** NASA's eye-tracking technology for docking spacecraft is now the standard for **LASIK eye surgery**, generating an estimated **$1.5 billion** in annual revenue.
- **Wearable Tech:** Biometric sensors for monitoring astronaut health laid the foundation for the **$36 billion global wearable market** (2020), expected to reach $114 billion by 2028.
- **Cardiology:** High-durability polymers (LaRC-SI) developed for aircraft are now standard insulators in **pacemakers**, a market valued at over **$4.5 billion**.

## 4. Funding Models and Market Shifts

- **Private vs. Public:** For the first time, **private commercial funding** has begun to surpass public investments in space, leading to "market logic" that reduces costs and development times.
- **Venture Capital:** Investment in space startups has grown from $0.1B/year (2006-2014) to an average of **$8B/year** today.
- **Cost Reductions:** NASA spinoff programs have reportedly led to **$6.2 billion in cost reductions** for terrestrial applications and saved over 444,000 lives.

## Key Takeaways

**High ROI**
Space investments can yield up to $40 per $1

**Medical Spinoffs**
Space R&D spawns multi-billion dollar Earth industries

**Private Funding Surge**
Venture investment has grown ~80x, leading funding

The concept of money in space is no longer about cost — it's about **value creation**. From ISRO's 2.54x returns to NASA's $40-per-dollar multiplier, from LASIK surgery to wearable tech, space and medical R&D investments are among the most powerful economic catalysts of our time.

## The Big Picture: Value Created

**$60B**
**ISRO Contribution**
To India's national economy over the last decade

**$6.2B**
**Cost Savings**
From NASA spinoff programmes for terrestrial applications

**444K+**
**Lives Saved**
Through medical and safety innovations from space technology

**$114B**
**Wearable Market**
Projected by 2028, rooted in astronaut biometric sensors

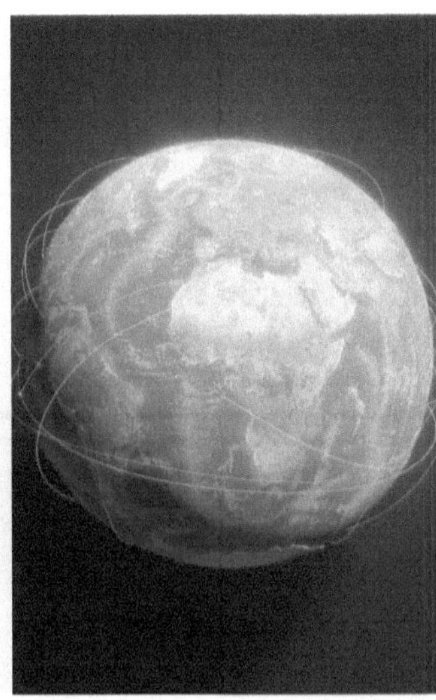

# The VC Space Investment Boom

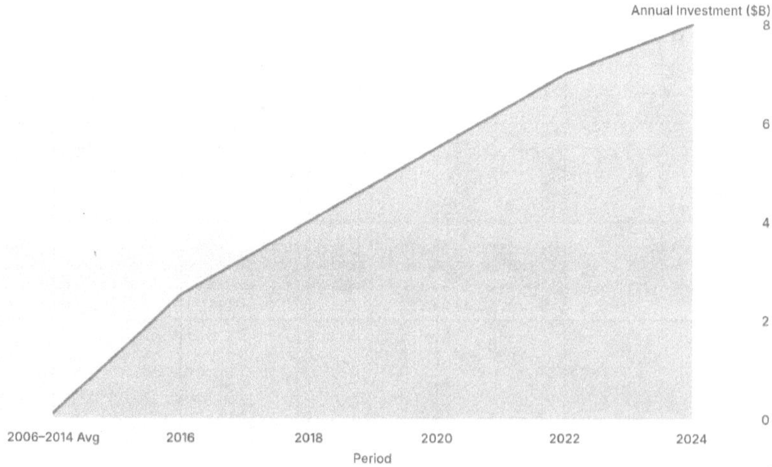


Venture capital investment in space startups has undergone a dramatic transformation — from a modest **$0.1 billion per year** during 2006–2014 to an average of **$8 billion per year** today. This shift signals that private markets now see space as a high-return investment frontier.

# The Wearable Tech Explosion

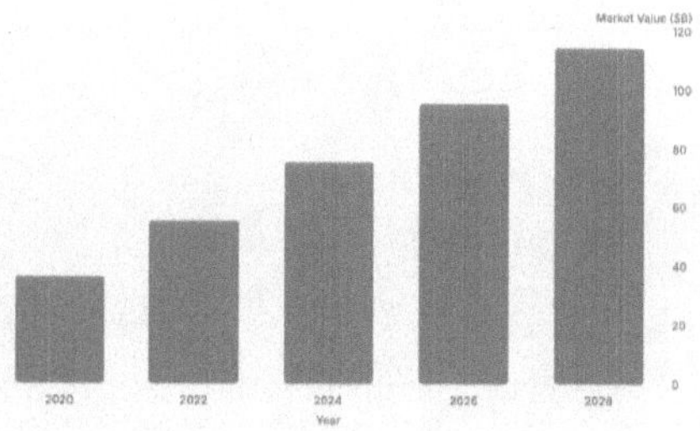


### From Astronaut Sensors to Your Wrist

Biometric sensors originally designed to monitor astronaut health in space have become the backbone of the global wearable technology market.

Growing from **$36 billion in 2020** to a projected **$114 billion by 2028**, this market exemplifies how space-born innovation creates massive commercial value on Earth.

## From Space Labs to Hospital Beds

Medical technologies developed for extreme space conditions often become **multi-billion dollar terrestrial industries**. Here are the most transformative spinoffs.

### Diagnostic Imaging

Digital image processing for moon landing photos directly led to the development of **MRI and CT scans**.

### Vision Correction

NASA's eye-tracking technology for docking spacecraft is now the standard for **LASIK surgery** — generating ~$1.5B in annual revenue.

### Wearable Tech

Biometric sensors for astronaut health laid the foundation for the **$36B global wearable market** (2020), expected to reach $114B by 2028.

### Cardiology

High-durability polymers (LaRC-SI) developed for aircraft are now standard insulators in **pacemakers** — a market valued at over $4.5B.

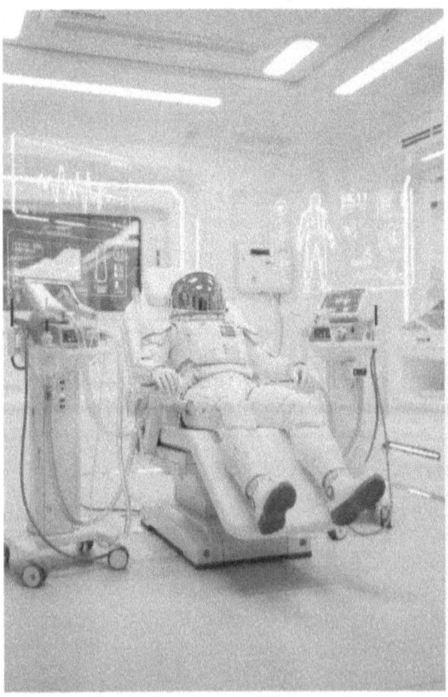

CHAPTER 3

# Medical Spinoffs as Commercial Assets

## A New Financial Principle: SVoM

The **Space Value of Money (SVoM)** proposes that space should be integrated as a foundational dimension of value in finance — creating entirely new monetary instruments and economic frameworks.

1

### Monetisation of Space

Creating money based on space-based value creation using new instruments like **Public Capitalisation Notes (PCNs)** for central bank funding.

2

### Space Currency

Concepts like the **"Quid"** have been designed to withstand space travel stresses, anticipating a future where electronic transfers are disrupted by astronomical distances.

3

### Cis-lunar Economy

The first phase will likely be based on **in-situ resource utilisation (ISRU)**, using lunar water and oxygen rather than shipping resources from Earth.

CHAPTER 2

# The "Space Value of Money"

## ISRO vs NASA: A Comparative View

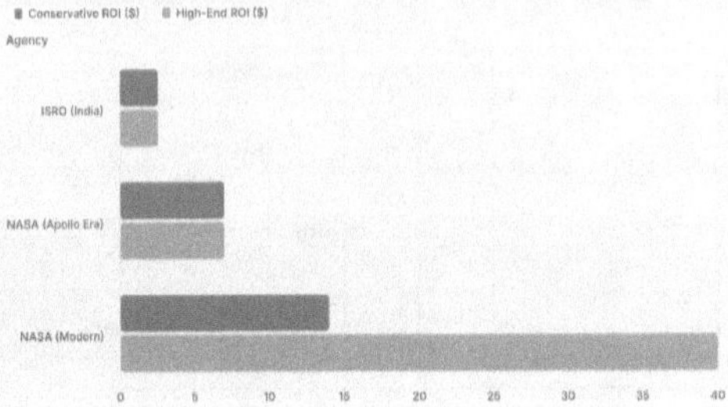


NASA's modern space development programmes yield up to **$40 for every $1 spent**, while ISRO delivers remarkable cost-efficiency with a 2.54x return on every rupee invested.

## Every Rupee and Dollar Multiplied

Space and medical R&D generate substantial financial returns by spinning off technologies into commercial markets. The numbers speak for themselves.

| 2.54x | $7–$40 | 12.5% |
|---|---|---|
| **ISRO Return** | **NASA ROI** | **CAGR** |
| Return on every rupee spent, contributing ~$60B to India's economy over the last decade | For every $1 spent — from the Apollo era to modern space development | Space medicine market growth, from $1.18B (2024) to $2.14B by 2029 |

CHAPTER 1

# Economic Multiplier & ROI

OVERVIEW

## From Expenditure to Economic Catalyst

Investments in space and medical R&D are increasingly viewed as powerful economic catalysts rather than mere expenditures. The "multiplier effect" on terrestrial industries transforms every rupee and dollar spent into exponential value — spinning off technologies, creating new markets, and saving lives.

### Traditional Cost Model

Space and medical R&D seen as government expenditure

### Paradigm Shift

Recognition of multiplier effects on commercial markets

### Value Creation

Investments generate multi-billion dollar returns across industries

# Money Beyond Earth

How space and medical technology investments are shifting from a "cost" model to a **value creation** framework — generating massive returns for terrestrial economies.

# 15

# Money, Finance and Blockchain Technology

In 2026, the intersection of money, finance, and blockchain has moved from speculative experimentation to becoming a core pillar of global financial infrastructure.

## The Digitalization of Money

- **Central Bank Digital Currencies (CBDCs)**: Over 130 countries are now exploring or piloting CBDCs, which are digital versions of national fiat currencies.
- Nations like China, India, and the EU are advancing programs to modernize payments and enhance financial inclusion.
- **Stablecoins as "The Internet's Dollar"**: These tokens, typically pegged 1:1 to assets like the US dollar, have become critical for instant 24/7 cross-border settlements.
- Stablecoin transaction volumes reached approximately $4 trillion in the first half of 2026, signalling massive mainstream adoption.

## Transformation of Financial Services

- **Asset Tokenization**: Trillions in traditional assets—including real estate, bonds, and equities—are being converted into digital tokens on blockchains.

- This "re-plumbing" allows for fractional ownership, meaning a single high-value asset can be owned by thousands of investors.
- **Institutional DeFi (Decentralized Finance)**: Traditional banks and asset managers are now integrating DeFi protocols for lending, borrowing, and yield generation.
- Major firms like BlackRock and JPMorgan have launched their own tokenization and blockchain-based settlement platforms.
- **Operational Efficiency**: Blockchain reduces the need for intermediaries, potentially saving the banking industry billions annually in cross-border fees and regulatory fines.
- Settlement times for international transfers have dropped from days to minutes or even seconds.

## Emerging Tech Synergies

- **AI and Blockchain Convergence**: Artificial Intelligence is now used to analyze blockchain data for real-time fraud detection and automated risk assessment.
- **Smart Contracts**: Self-executing agreements are automating complex workflows in insurance, trade finance, and supply chains, reducing human error and administrative costs.

## Regulatory and Security Landscape

- **Global Regulatory Clarity**: Major frameworks like Europe's **MiCA** and the US **GENIUS Act** (passed in late 2025/2026) have established clear rules for digital assets, boosting institutional confidence.
- **Scalability and Sustainability**: Networks have largely shifted to energy-efficient consensus models like Proof of Stake, significantly reducing the environmental impact of blockchain technology.

## Key Takeaways

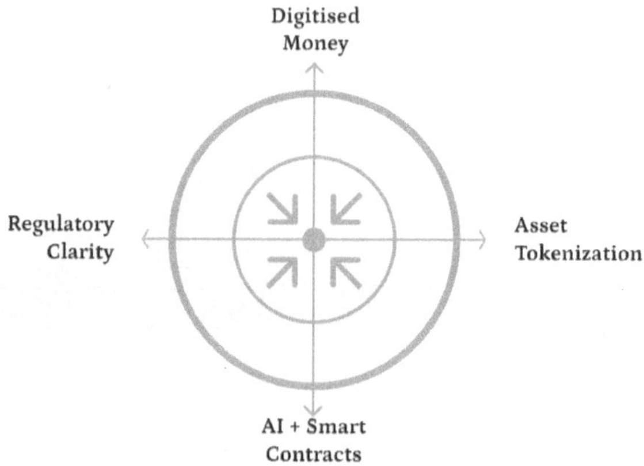


In 2026, blockchain is no longer speculative — it is the backbone of a faster, more inclusive, and more efficient global financial system.

## Scalability & Sustainability

Blockchain networks have largely shifted to energy-efficient consensus models like **Proof of Stake**, significantly reducing the environmental impact of the technology.

This transition addresses one of the most persistent criticisms of blockchain — its energy consumption — making the technology viable for sustainable, large-scale deployment across global finance.

## Global Regulatory Clarity

Major regulatory frameworks have established clear rules for digital assets, boosting institutional confidence and accelerating adoption worldwide.

**Europe's MiCA**

Markets in Crypto-Assets regulation providing comprehensive EU-wide framework for digital asset issuance and trading

**US GENIUS Act**

Passed in late 2025/2026, establishing clear stablecoin and digital asset rules for the American market

CHAPTER 4

# Regulatory & Security Landscape

## Smart Contracts Automating Industries

Self-executing agreements are automating complex workflows across multiple sectors, reducing human error and administrative costs significantly.

### Insurance

Automated claims processing and instant payouts triggered by verified events

### Trade Finance

Letters of credit and payment guarantees executed without manual intervention

### Supply Chains

End-to-end tracking with automatic payments upon delivery confirmation

## AI & Blockchain Convergence

### The Power Combination

Artificial intelligence is now used to analyse blockchain data for **real-time fraud detection** and **automated risk assessment** — creating a security layer that evolves and improves continuously.

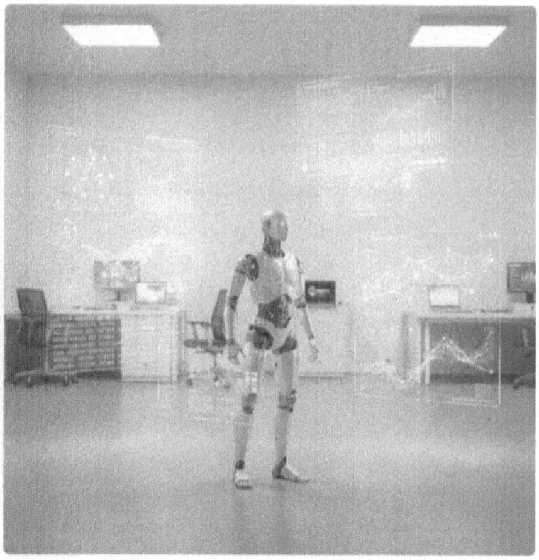

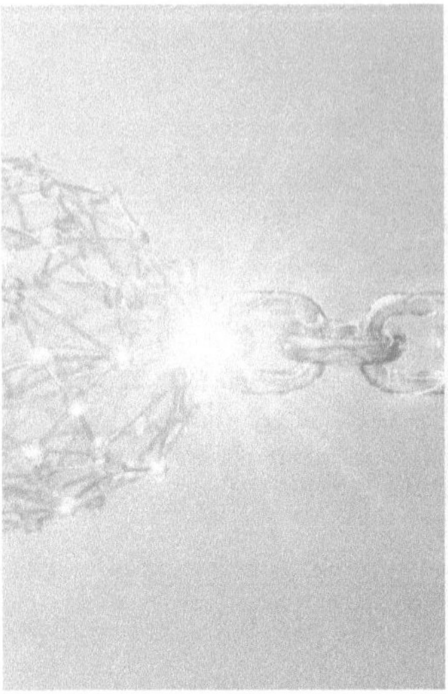

CHAPTER 3

# Emerging Tech Synergies

## Operational Efficiency Gains

Blockchain reduces the need for intermediaries, potentially saving the banking industry **billions annually** in cross-border fees and regulatory fines.

### Before Blockchain

International transfers took **days** with multiple intermediaries

### With Blockchain

Settlement times dropped to **minutes or seconds**

## Institutional DeFi

Traditional banks and asset managers are now integrating **Decentralised Finance (DeFi)** protocols for lending, borrowing, and yield generation — bridging the gap between legacy finance and blockchain innovation.

### BlackRock

Launched tokenization platforms for institutional-grade digital asset management

### JPMorgan

Deployed blockchain-based settlement platforms for cross-border transactions

These moves by major firms signal that DeFi is no longer experimental — it's becoming standard financial infrastructure.

## Asset Tokenization

Trillions in traditional assets — including real estate, bonds, and equities — are being converted into digital tokens on blockchains. This "re-plumbing" of finance allows for **fractional ownership**, meaning a single high-value asset can be owned by thousands of investors.

### Real Estate

Properties divided into thousands of tradeable digital tokens

### Bonds

Fixed-income instruments settled on-chain in minutes, not days

### Equities

Fractional share ownership accessible to global investors 24/7

CHAPTER 2

# Transformation of Financial Services

## Stablecoins: "The Internet's Dollar"

Stablecoins — tokens pegged 1:1 to assets like the US dollar — have become critical infrastructure for instant, 24/7 cross-border settlements.

Transaction volumes reached approximately **$4 trillion** in the first half of 2026 alone, signalling massive mainstream adoption far beyond crypto-native users.

Stablecoins now process more value than many traditional payment networks, operating around the clock without banking hours or holidays.

## Central Bank Digital Currencies (CBDCs)

Over **130 countries** are now exploring or piloting CBDCs — digital versions of national fiat currencies designed to modernise payments and enhance financial inclusion.

### China

Digital yuan expanding across domestic and cross-border payments

### India

Digital rupee pilot scaling to millions of retail users

### European Union

Digital euro programme advancing toward full deployment

CHAPTER 1

# The Digitalization of Money

## What We'll Cover

01

**The Digitalization of Money**

CBDCs, stablecoins, and the new architecture of payments

02

**Transformation of Financial Services**

Asset tokenization, institutional DeFi, and operational efficiency

03

**Emerging Tech Synergies**

AI convergence and smart contract automation

04

**Regulatory & Security Landscape**

Global frameworks and sustainable blockchain networks

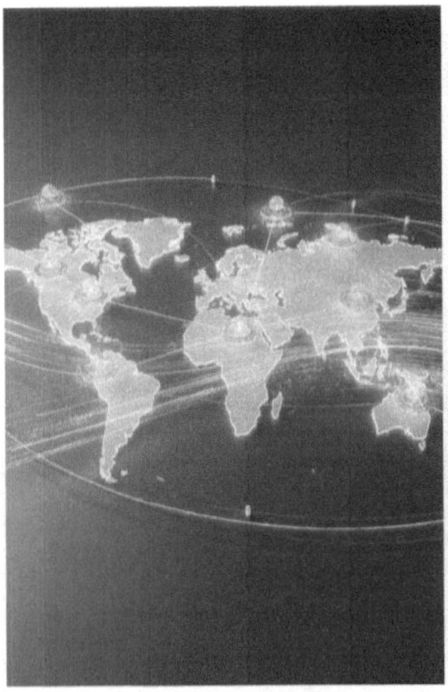

## Money, Finance & Blockchain in 2026

How blockchain has evolved from speculative experimentation to a core pillar of global financial infrastructure.

# 16

# Monetary Policy and International Financing Through Organizations

Monetary policy and international financing through organizations like the **International Monetary Fund (IMF)** and the World Bank are deeply interconnected through the stabilization of the global economy and the provision of liquidity during crises. While central banks manage domestic price stability and interest rates, international organizations provide a framework for cooperation and financial safety nets to prevent systemic failures.

## 1. The Role of International Organizations in Financing

- **International Monetary Fund (IMF)**: Acts as the "lender of last resort" for member countries experiencing **balance of payments** (BOP) difficulties.
    - **Financial Assistance**: Provides short- to medium-term loans to help countries replenish international reserves and stabilize their currencies.
    - **Special Drawing Rights (SDRs)**: Issues an international reserve asset to provide members with additional liquidity without increasing debt.

- **World Bank Group**: Focuses on long-term economic development and poverty reduction in developing nations.
    - **Project Financing**: Provides low-interest loans and grants for infrastructure, health, and education projects.
    - **Market Borrowing**: The IBRD (part of the World Bank) issues AAA-rated bonds in global capital markets to fund these developmental loans.

## 2. Interaction Between Financing and Monetary Policy

- **Policy Conditionality**: Financing from organizations like the IMF often requires recipient countries to implement specific monetary reforms, such as **tightening interest rates** to control inflation or devaluing their currency to restore competitiveness.
- **Catalytic Effect**: Official financing can act as a signal of credibility, boosting investor confidence and attracting additional private capital flows, which can lead to currency appreciation.
- **Exchange Rate Regimes**: A country's monetary policy is limited by its exchange rate regime; those with fixed rates must often coordinate more closely with international bodies to maintain parity.
- **Spillover Management**: Major economies' monetary decisions (e.g., U.S. Federal Reserve interest rate hikes) create global spillovers; international organizations facilitate the monitoring and coordination needed to mitigate these cross-border effects.

## 3. Global Monetary Policy Coordination

- **Surveillance**: The IMF conducts regular "Article IV" consultations to monitor the economic health of its 190 member nations and advise on sustainable monetary strategies.

- **Standard Setting**: Organizations like the **Bank for International Settlements (BIS)** and the **Financial Stability Board (FSB)** coordinate with central banks to establish global regulatory standards, such as capital requirements, to ensure financial stability.
- **Swap Facilities**: During crises, central banks often establish currency swap lines—sometimes coordinated or supported by international frameworks—to provide immediate foreign exchange liquidity.

## Key Takeaways

**IMF as Safety Net**

Acts as lender of last resort, providing loans and SDRs to stabilise currencies and replenish reserves.

**World Bank for Development**

Funds long-term infrastructure, health, and education through low-interest loans and AAA-rated bonds.

**Policy Conditionality**

International financing shapes domestic monetary reforms, from interest rate adjustments to currency devaluation.

**Global Coordination**

Surveillance, standard-setting, and swap facilities ensure cross-border stability and mitigate spillover effects.

## How It All Connects

The interplay between domestic monetary policy, international financing, and global coordination creates a resilient framework that underpins the stability of the world economy.

## Three Pillars of Coordination

### Surveillance

The IMF conducts regular **"Article IV" consultations** to monitor the economic health of its 190 member nations and advise on sustainable monetary strategies.

### Standard Setting

The **BIS** and **Financial Stability Board (FSB)** coordinate with central banks to establish global regulatory standards, such as capital requirements, ensuring financial stability.

### Swap Facilities

During crises, central banks establish **currency swap lines** — often coordinated by international frameworks — to provide immediate foreign exchange liquidity.

CHAPTER 3

# Global Monetary Policy Coordination

Beyond crisis response, international organisations play a vital ongoing role in surveillance, standard-setting, and emergency liquidity provision to keep the global financial system stable.

# Exchange Rates & Spillover Management

### Exchange Rate Regimes

A country's monetary policy is limited by its exchange rate regime. Those with **fixed rates** must coordinate more closely with international bodies to maintain parity, constraining their domestic policy options.

### Spillover Management

Major economies' monetary decisions — such as **U.S. Federal Reserve interest rate hikes** — create global spillovers. International organisations facilitate the monitoring and coordination needed to mitigate these cross-border effects.

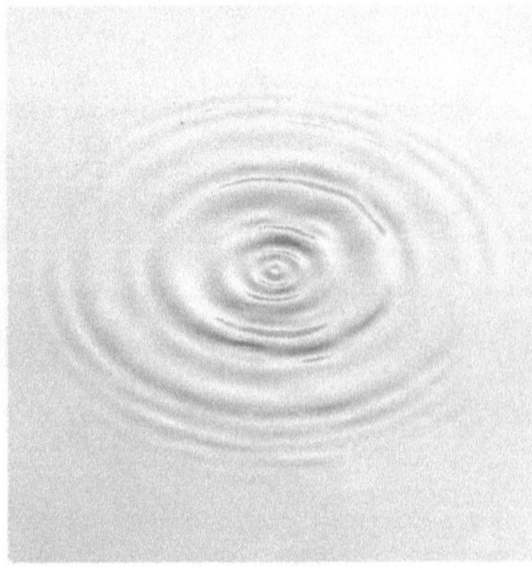

# How Financing Shapes Monetary Policy

### Policy Conditionality

IMF financing often requires recipient countries to implement specific monetary reforms — tightening interest rates to control inflation or devaluing currency to restore competitiveness.

### Catalytic Effect

Official financing acts as a signal of credibility, boosting investor confidence and attracting additional private capital flows, which can lead to currency appreciation.

CHAPTER 2

# Interaction Between Financing & Monetary Policy

International financing and domestic monetary policy are not isolated — they influence and constrain each other in powerful ways.

## World Bank Group

The World Bank focuses on **long-term economic development** and **poverty reduction** in developing nations, channelling resources into projects that transform communities.

1 **Project Financing**

Provides low-interest loans and grants for infrastructure, health, and education projects in developing economies.

2 **Market Borrowing**

The IBRD (part of the World Bank) issues **AAA-rated bonds** in global capital markets to fund these developmental loans.

# International Monetary Fund (IMF)

The IMF acts as the **"lender of last resort"** for member countries experiencing balance of payments (BOP) difficulties, providing critical financial lifelines when nations face currency or liquidity crises.

### Financial Assistance

Provides short- to medium-term loans to help countries replenish international reserves and stabilise their currencies.

### Special Drawing Rights (SDRs)

Issues an international reserve asset to provide members with additional liquidity without increasing debt.

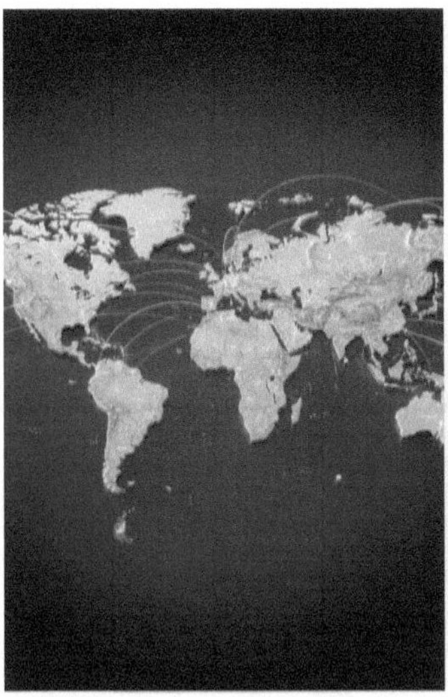

CHAPTER 1

# The Role of International Organisations in Financing

International organisations serve as the backbone of global financial stability, each fulfilling a distinct mandate — from emergency lending to long-term development.

OVERVIEW

## The Global Financial Architecture

Monetary policy and international financing are deeply interconnected through the stabilisation of the global economy and the provision of liquidity during crises.

While **central banks** manage domestic price stability and interest rates, **international organisations** provide a framework for cooperation and financial safety nets to prevent systemic failures.

**Key Pillars**

- Domestic monetary management
- International financial cooperation
- Crisis prevention & response
- Long-term development financing

## Monetary Policy & International Financing

How the IMF, World Bank, and central banks work together to stabilise the global economy and provide liquidity during crises.

# 17

# Block Chian Economy

The blockchain economy in 2026 is transitioning from an era of retail-driven speculation to a foundational "Institutional Era" defined by real-world asset (RWA) tokenization, regulatory clarity, and deep integration with traditional finance (TradFi).

## Market Dynamics & Forecasts

- **Rapid Growth**: The global blockchain technology market is projected to reach between **$39.82 billion** and **$47.96 billion** in 2026.
- **Institutional Shift**: Institutional capital is replacing retail momentum, leading to steadier price advances for major assets like Bitcoin and Ethereum.
- **Tokenization Explosion**: RWAs (real estate, bonds, private credit) on-chain are expected to surpass **$50 billion** in 2026, up from $18.5 billion in 2025.
- **Stablecoin Maturity**: Stablecoins have become essential financial infrastructure, with monthly transaction volumes reaching **$1.1 trillion** as they integrate into corporate balance sheets and cross-border payments.

## Key Sector Analysis

- **Finance (BFSI)**: Remains the dominant sector, accounting for roughly **23.5% to 41%** of total market revenue.
    - Banks are shifting from experimentation to "on-chain" operations for 24/7 clearing and settlement.
- **Healthcare**: Projected to be the fastest-growing non-financial sector through 2030, focusing on secure clinical data exchange and patient-centric identity.
- **Supply Chain**: Blockchain is now a requirement for transparency in luxury goods and pharmaceuticals to combat counterfeiting.
- **Artificial Intelligence**: AI and blockchain are converging, with blockchain providing a verifiable "paper trail" for AI decision-making and decentralized compute markets.

## Structural & Regulatory Landscape

- **Regulatory Clarity**: Major laws like the **U.S. GENIUS Act** (for stablecoins) and the **EU's MiCA** (enforced since 2025) are providing the legal certainty necessary for Fortune 500 adoption.
- **Invisible Infrastructure**: Technology is becoming "invisible" to end-users, integrated into the back-end of standard applications via "Wallet-as-a-Service" (WaaS).
- **Sustainability**: The industry has largely pivoted to energy-efficient consensus mechanisms (Proof of Stake), with "green" blockchains reducing energy consumption by over 99% compared to older systems.

## Emerging Trends for 2026

- **Central Bank Digital Currencies (CBDCs)**: Over 20 countries, including India, China, and the EU, are expected to have operational or advanced pilot CBDCs by 2026.
- **Layer-2 Dominance**: Scaling solutions (rollups, sidechains) are now the primary layer for consumer apps, drastically reducing transaction fees and latency.
- **Modular Architecture**: Networks are decoupling core functions (consensus, data availability), allowing businesses to build cheaper, specialized chains.

## Key Takeaways

1 **Institutional Era**

Blockchain has moved beyond retail speculation — institutional capital and TradFi integration are driving steady, sustainable growth.

2 **Tokenization is Real**

RWAs on-chain surpassing **$50 billion** and stablecoin volumes at **$1.1 trillion/month** prove blockchain's utility in real-world finance.

3 **Regulation Enables Growth**

The U.S. GENIUS Act and EU's MiCA provide the legal certainty that Fortune 500 companies need to adopt blockchain at scale.

4 **Infrastructure Goes Invisible**

From WaaS to Layer-2 scaling and modular chains, blockchain is becoming seamless, sustainable, and ready for mass adoption.

## The Road Ahead: 2026 at a Glance

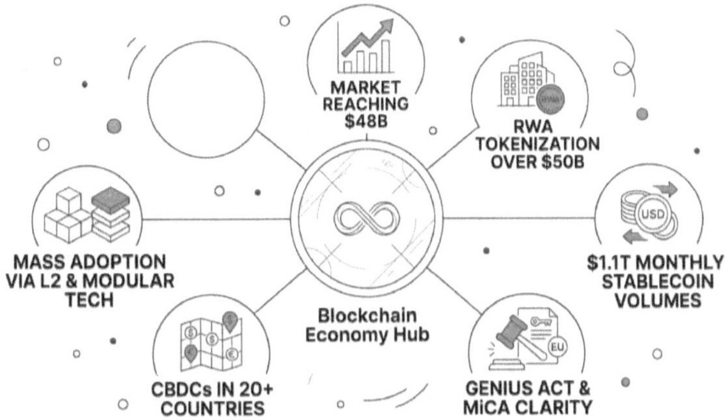


The blockchain economy in 2026 stands at an inflection point — institutional capital, regulatory frameworks, and invisible infrastructure are converging to make blockchain a foundational layer of the global financial system.

## Layer-2 Dominance & Modular Architecture

The technical infrastructure of blockchain is evolving rapidly, with two trends reshaping how applications are built and scaled.

### Layer-2 Scaling

Rollups and sidechains are now the **primary layer** for consumer apps, drastically reducing transaction fees and latency.

### Modular Architecture

Networks are decoupling core functions — consensus, data availability — allowing businesses to build **cheaper, specialised chains**.

### Mass Adoption

Together, these innovations make blockchain fast, affordable, and customisable enough for mainstream enterprise use.

## CBDCs Go Global

Over **20 countries,** including India, China, and the EU, are expected to have operational or advanced pilot Central Bank Digital Currencies by 2026. This represents a fundamental shift in how sovereign money is issued and distributed.

### India

Digital Rupee pilot expanding

### China

e-CNY in advanced rollout

### EU

Digital Euro in pilot phase

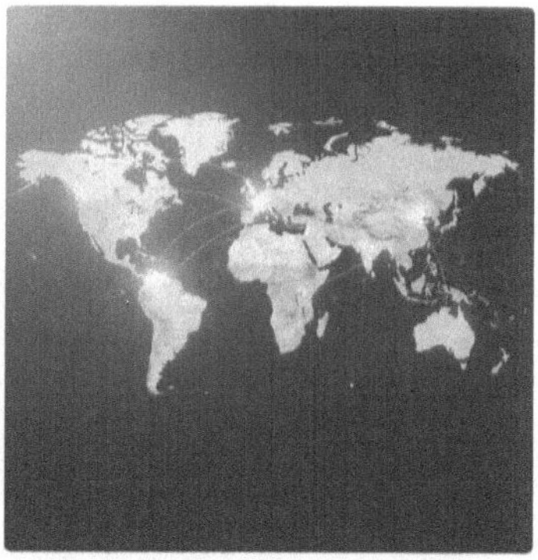

CHAPTER 4 EMERGING TRENDS FOR 2026

# Emerging Trends for 2026

## Invisible Infrastructure & Sustainability

### Invisible to End-Users

Blockchain technology is becoming "invisible," integrated into the back-end of standard applications via **"Wallet-as-a-Service" (WaaS)**. Users interact with blockchain without knowing it.

### Green Blockchains

The industry has largely pivoted to energy-efficient Proof of Stake consensus mechanisms. "Green" blockchains reduce energy consumption by **over 99%** compared to older systems.

## Regulatory Clarity Unlocks Adoption

Major legislation is providing the legal certainty necessary for Fortune 500 adoption, transforming blockchain from a grey-area technology into a regulated, enterprise-ready infrastructure.

### U.S. GENIUS Act

Landmark stablecoin legislation providing a clear regulatory framework for issuance, reserves, and compliance in the United States.

### EU's MiCA

Markets in Crypto-Assets regulation enforced since 2025, establishing comprehensive rules for crypto-asset service providers across Europe.

### Fortune 500 Confidence

Legal certainty from these frameworks is enabling major corporations to integrate blockchain into core operations without regulatory risk.

CHAPTER 3 STRUCTURAL & REGULATORY LANDSCAPE

## Structural & Regulatory Landscape

# BFSI Market Dominance

The finance sector's share of blockchain revenue underscores how deeply the technology has embedded itself into traditional financial operations.

> ☐ Banks are no longer experimenting — they are running **production-grade on-chain operations** for 24/7 clearing and settlement, fundamentally changing how capital markets function.

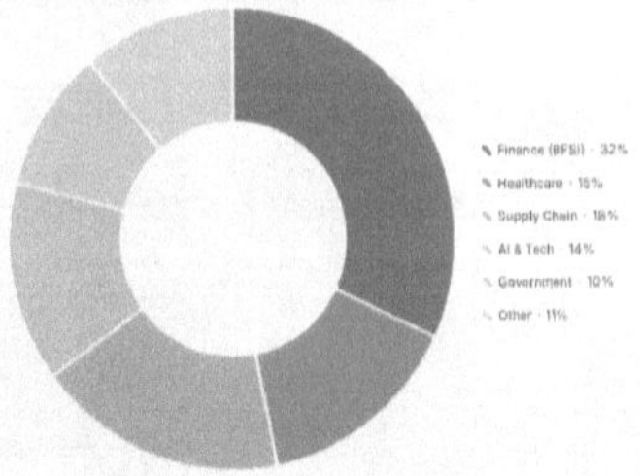


BFSI accounts for roughly **23.5% to 41%** of total blockchain market revenue, depending on the estimate.

# Finance Leads, Healthcare Accelerates

The BFSI sector remains dominant, accounting for roughly **23.5% to 41%** of total market revenue. Banks are shifting from experimentation to full "on-chain" operations for 24/7 clearing and settlement.

### Finance (BFSI)

Dominant sector at **23.5–41%** of revenue. Banks moving to on-chain 24/7 clearing and settlement.

### Healthcare

Fastest-growing non-financial sector through 2030. Focus on secure clinical data exchange and patient-centric identity.

### Supply Chain

Now a requirement for transparency in luxury goods and pharmaceuticals to combat counterfeiting.

### AI Convergence

Blockchain provides a verifiable "paper trail" for AI decision-making and decentralised compute markets.

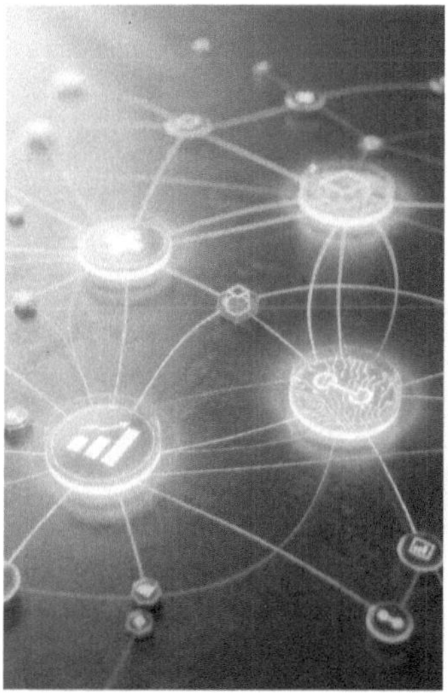

CHAPTER 2 KEY SECTOR ANALYSIS

# Key Sector Analysis

## Tokenization & Stablecoin Explosion

### Tokenization Surge

RWAs — including real estate, bonds, and private credit — on-chain are expected to surpass **$50 billion** in 2026, up from $18.5 billion in 2025. This represents a near **3x growth** in just one year.

### Stablecoin Maturity

Stablecoins have become essential financial infrastructure, with monthly transaction volumes reaching **$1.1 trillion**. They are now integrated into corporate balance sheets and cross-border payments at scale.

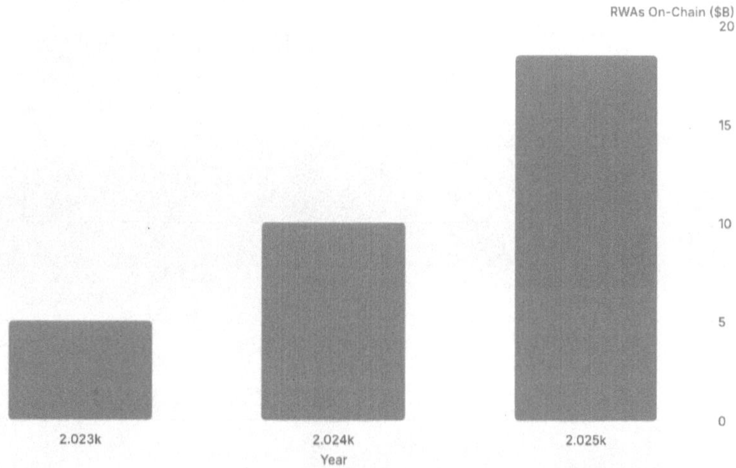


RWA tokenization is on an exponential trajectory, with 2026 marking a pivotal inflection point for institutional adoption.

## A Market Surging Toward $48 Billion

The global blockchain technology market is projected to reach between **$39.82 billion** and **$47.96 billion** in 2026, driven by institutional capital replacing retail momentum. This shift is leading to steadier price advances for major assets like Bitcoin and Ethereum.

| $48B | $50B+ | $1.1T |
|---|---|---|
| **Market Size** | **RWAs On-Chain** | **Stablecoin Volume** |
| Upper projection for global blockchain market in 2026 | Real estate, bonds, and private credit tokenized — up from $18.5B in 2025 | Monthly transaction volume as stablecoins become essential financial infrastructure |

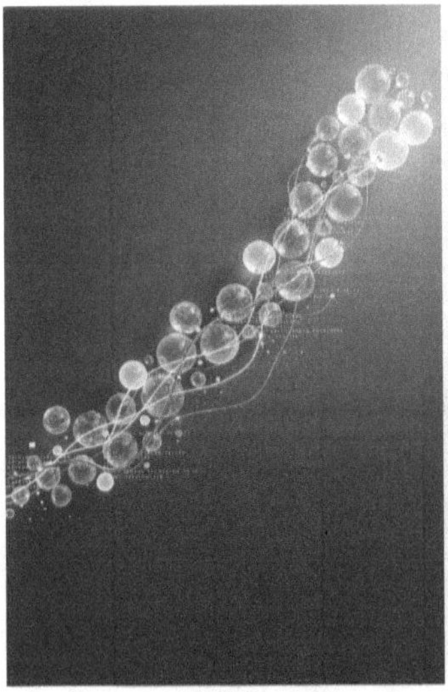

CHAPTER 1 · MARKET DYNAMICS & FORECASTS

## Market Dynamics & Forecasts

OVERVIEW

## The Great Transition

The blockchain economy in 2026 is transitioning from an era of retail-driven speculation to a foundational **"Institutional Era"** defined by three pillars:

### RWA Tokenization

Real-world assets moving on-chain at unprecedented scale

### Regulatory Clarity

Landmark legislation enabling Fortune 500 adoption

### TradFi Integration

Deep convergence with traditional financial infrastructure

## The Blockchain Economy in 2026

From retail speculation to the **Institutional Era** — defined by real-world asset tokenization, regulatory clarity, and deep integration with traditional finance.

# 18

# How Quantum Cryptography Could Be a Game Changer for Decentralised Financing

Quantum cryptography is a transformative shift for **decentralised finance (DeFi)**, moving security from mathematical assumptions to the fundamental **laws of physics**. While today's DeFi relies on algorithms like RSA and ECC—which are vulnerable to quantum attacks—quantum-based protocols offer "unbreakable" alternatives.

## 1. Eliminating Key Vulnerabilities

Current DeFi platforms use asymmetric cryptography for digital signatures and wallet keys.

- **Shor's Algorithm Threat**: A sufficiently powerful quantum computer could use Shor's algorithm to derive private keys from public ones, allowing attackers to drain any wallet.
- **Quantum-Safe Solutions**: Technologies like **Quantum Key Distribution (QKD)** generate keys using photons. Any attempt to intercept the key disturbs its quantum state, alerting users and making it physically impossible to "harvest" keys for later decryption.

## 2. Reinforcing Immutability and Consensus

Quantum principles can redesign how decentralised networks reach agreement.

- **Quantum Proof-of-Stake (QPoS)**: New frameworks tie block validation to "entanglement fidelity" rather than just financial stake, making fraud or double-spending physically impossible due to the **no-cloning theorem**.
- **Consensus Speed**: Entanglement-assisted consensus can reduce communication overhead from to, potentially increasing transaction throughput by up to **90%** compared to classical protocols.

## 3. Native Quantum Assets

DeFi could move beyond "tokenized" classical assets to **quantum-native assets**.

- **Unclonable Money**: Based on Wiesner's quantum money theory, these assets are physically impossible to counterfeit or duplicate.
- **True Randomness**: **Quantum Random Number Generators (QRNG)** provide "pure" unpredictability for on-chain events like validator elections or lottery protocols, removing the bias risks of classical pseudo-randomness.

## 4. Implementation Hurdles

Despite the potential, significant barriers remain for widespread DeFi adoption:

- **Infrastructure Costs**: QKD requires specialized hardware like fiber-optic quantum channels or satellites (e.g., China's Micius), which are currently far more expensive than software-based solutions.

- **Decentralisation Conflict**: Most current QKD systems rely on "trusted nodes" or centralized hardware hubs, which may conflict with the core "trustless" ethos of DeFi.
- **Network Limits**: Terrestrial QKD is currently limited to a few hundred kilometers without "quantum repeaters," a technology still in experimental stages.

## Analysis Summary: Classical vs. Quantum Blockchain

| Feature | Classical DeFi | Quantum-Enhanced DeFi |
|---|---|---|
| **Security Basis** | Mathematical complexity | Laws of quantum physics |
| **Key Threat** | Breakable by Shor's algorithm | Immune to quantum cryptanalysis |
| **Randomness** | Pseudo-random (algorithmic) | Truly random (physical) |
| **Infrastructure** | Standard internet/ hardware | Specialized quantum hardware |
| **Scalability** | Limited by consensus | entanglement-based speed |

## The Road Ahead

Quantum cryptography promises to redefine DeFi security — shifting from breakable mathematical assumptions to the **unbreakable laws of physics**. While infrastructure costs, decentralisation conflicts, and network limits present real hurdles, the potential rewards are extraordinary: unclonable assets, tamper-proof consensus, and truly random on-chain events.

> The question is not *if* quantum cryptography will reshape DeFi — but *when* the infrastructure catches up with the physics.

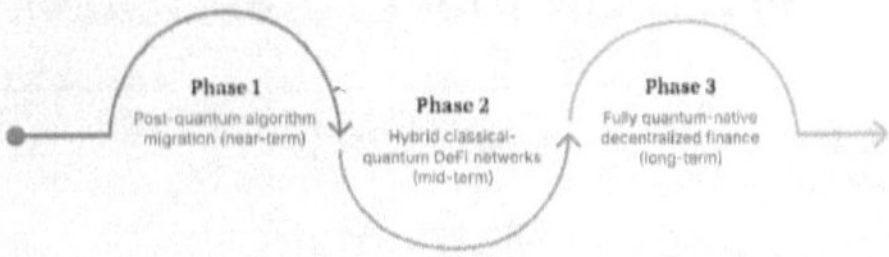


Organisations that begin preparing now — adopting quantum-resistant algorithms and monitoring QKD advances — will be best positioned for the quantum era of decentralised finance.

## The Quantum Advantage at a Glance

| 90% | 0% | 100% |
|---|---|---|
| Throughput Gain | Cloning Risk | True Randomness |
| Potential increase via entanglement-assisted consensus | No-cloning theorem makes duplication physically impossible | QRNG delivers pure unpredictability from quantum physics |

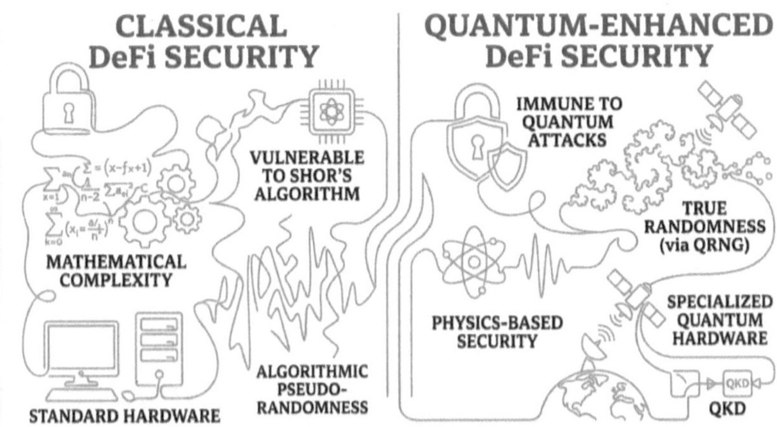

## Classical vs. Quantum-Enhanced DeFi

A side-by-side comparison reveals the paradigm shift quantum cryptography brings to blockchain security and performance.

| Feature | Classical DeFi | Quantum-Enhanced DeFi |
|---|---|---|
| Security Basis | Mathematical complexity | Laws of quantum physics |
| Key Threat | Breakable by Shor's algorithm | Immune to quantum cryptanalysis |
| Randomness | Pseudo-random (algorithmic) | Truly random (physical) |
| Infrastructure | Standard internet/hardware | Specialised quantum hardware |
| Scalability | Limited by classical consensus | Entanglement-based speed |

△ CHALLENGES

## Implementation Hurdles

Despite the potential, significant barriers remain for widespread DeFi adoption of quantum cryptography.

1

### Infrastructure Costs

QKD requires specialised hardware like fibre-optic quantum channels or satellites (e.g., China's **Micius**), far more expensive than software-based solutions.

2

### Decentralisation Conflict

Most current QKD systems rely on **"trusted nodes"** or centralised hardware hubs, conflicting with DeFi's core "trustless" ethos.

3

### Network Limits

Terrestrial QKD is limited to a **few hundred kilometres** without "quantum repeaters" — a technology still in experimental stages.

CHAPTER 3

# Native Quantum Assets

DeFi could move beyond "tokenized" classical assets to **quantum-native assets** — a fundamentally new class of digital value.

### Unclonable Money

Based on **Wiesner's quantum money theory**, these assets are physically impossible to counterfeit or duplicate — true digital scarcity enforced by physics.

### True Randomness (QRNG)

**Quantum Random Number Generators** provide "pure" unpredictability for on-chain events like validator elections or lottery protocols, removing bias risks of classical pseudo-randomness.

CHAPTER 2

# Reinforcing Immutability & Consensus

Quantum principles can fundamentally redesign how decentralised networks reach agreement, making fraud physically impossible.

### Quantum Proof-of-Stake (QPoS)

New frameworks tie block validation to **"entanglement fidelity"** rather than just financial stake. The **no-cloning theorem** makes fraud or double-spending physically impossible.

### Consensus Speed

Entanglement-assisted consensus can reduce communication overhead dramatically, potentially increasing **transaction throughput by up to 90%** compared to classical protocols.

## Quantum Key Distribution (QKD)

Quantum-safe solutions like **Quantum Key Distribution** generate keys using photons. Any attempt to intercept the key disturbs its quantum state, **alerting users immediately** and making it physically impossible to "harvest" keys for later decryption.

**Photon Key Generation**
Keys encoded in quantum states of light

**Eavesdrop Detection**
Interception disturbs quantum state

**Secure Communication**
Physically unbreakable key exchange

## The Quantum Threat to Current DeFi

Current DeFi platforms use **asymmetric cryptography** for digital signatures and wallet keys. This creates a critical vulnerability:

- **Shor's Algorithm Threat:** A sufficiently powerful quantum computer could use Shor's algorithm to derive private keys from public ones, allowing attackers to **drain any wallet**.

This means every wallet, every smart contract, and every digital signature in today's DeFi ecosystem is potentially at risk once large-scale quantum computers become a reality.

OVERVIEW

## Why Quantum Cryptography Matters for DeFi

Quantum cryptography represents a transformative shift for decentralised finance. While today's DeFi relies on algorithms like RSA and ECC—which are vulnerable to quantum attacks—quantum-based protocols offer **"unbreakable" alternatives** rooted in the laws of physics rather than computational difficulty.

01

**Eliminating Key Vulnerabilities**

Quantum-safe key distribution

02

**Reinforcing Consensus**

Entanglement-based validation

03

**Native Quantum Assets**

Unclonable digital money

04

**Implementation Hurdles**

Infrastructure & scalability challenges

## Quantum Cryptography & the Future of DeFi

Moving decentralised finance security from mathematical assumptions to the fundamental laws of physics.

# Conclusion

In **conclusion**, money has evolved from a simple commodity of exchange into a sophisticated instrument of state power and social mobility. By functioning as **legal tender**, it provides the standardized framework necessary for a stable economy, backed by the authority of the state rather than intrinsic physical value.

While the shift toward **centralized fiat currency** introduces risks like inflation, its role in maintaining economic order and facilitating global trade remains unparalleled. Ultimately, money is more than just a medium of exchange; it is a vital tool for **socio-economic transformation**, allowing individuals to break the cycle of poverty by investing in human capital and long-term stability. As we move into the era of **digital currencies**, the fundamental value of money will continue to depend on the balance between government-led stability and the evolving needs of a globalized society.

# About the Author

The author Subhradeep Sarkar, is a civil servant, internal auditor, AI based digital content creator and a finance enthusiast and author of 10 HABITS THAT WILL MAKE YOU RICH with a Master degree holder in Science. He has rich experience in public service and social welfare. He has expertise on social welfare and institutional auditing as well as in financial instruments. Currently working under a Government administration in West Bengal, India.

Social media links:

Facebook: Facebook.subhradeep.sarkar.3

Facebook page: AI Finance

Instagram: subhradeeps78

Youtube link: SUBHRADEEPSARKAR78

e-mail: subhradeeps78@gmail.com

www.ingramcontent.com/pod-product-compliance
Lightning Source LLC
La Vergne TN
LVHW090406210926
848480LV00002B/474
*9798903429431*